The TOWER of LONDON

The TOWER of LONDON

The OFFICIAL *Illustrated* HISTORY

EDWARD IMPEY and GEOFFREY PARNELL

MERRELL
in association with
HISTORIC ROYAL PALACES

The TOWER *of* LONDON

The OFFICIAL *Illustrated* HISTORY

CONTENTS

PART 2 The TOWER and its INSTITUTIONS 1485–2000

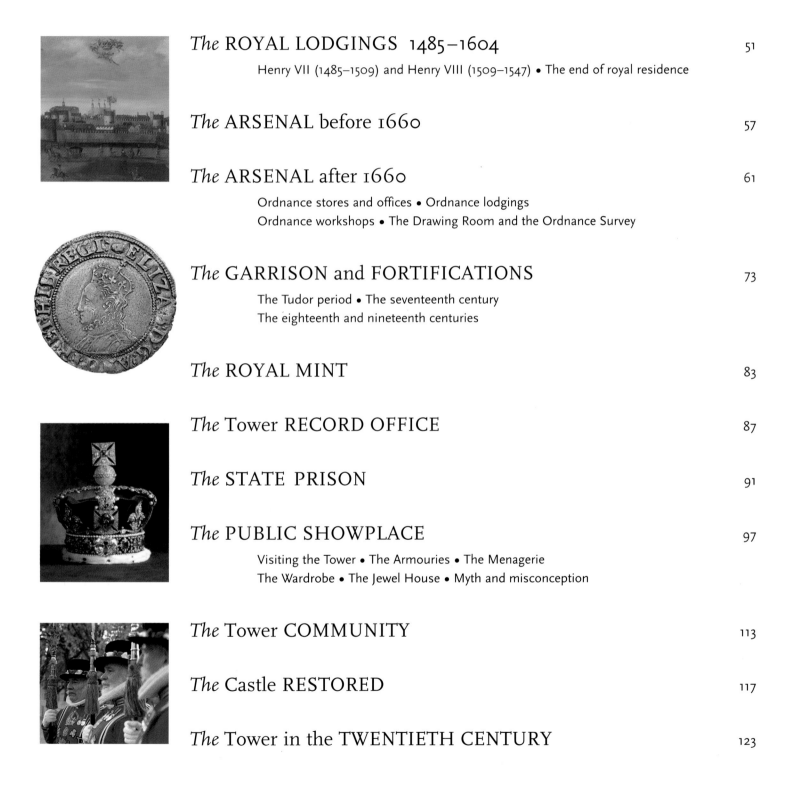

Den Tower van London

Introduction

THE TOWER OF LONDON is one of the most famous and most visited historic monuments in the world. For most people it conjures up images of Norman architecture and towering battlements, but predominantly of arms and armour, ravens, the Crown Jewels, the Yeoman Warders, imprisonment, torture and death. But this is not, of course, to do it justice: the history of the Tower and its buildings is a vast, fascinating and complex subject, intertwined with the history of the country, its government, its kings and queens, its people and its institutions. The myths that surround the Tower's history reflect this, and are of interest in themselves, but the truth – as so often – is stranger than the fiction.

This book is intended to present an outline of the Tower's story from its foundation early in the last millennium to the present day. The complexity of the subject and the nature both of the Tower's history and of what we know about it has made it appropriate to present it in two parts. The castle's first four centuries saw the development, in most essentials, of the layout that we know today. They saw, too, its apogee as a great fortress and the high point in its use as a royal residence. But of the various activities and institutions that later came to dominate the Tower we know relatively little with regard to this period. The first section of the book, 'The Tower in the Middle Ages', is therefore arranged chronologically, describing the development of the Tower's buildings, with some reference to associated events and personalities.

From the late fifteenth century onwards, however, the picture changes. As the Tower's role as a fortress declined, both the importance of the activities and institutions that it had fostered, and the amount we know about them, vastly increases. The second part, 'The Tower and its Institutions 1485–2000', is therefore not approached strictly chronologically, but brings out the Tower's history in a series of chapters on these various institutions and activities, along with others on particular aspects of the castle's life and its development in this period.

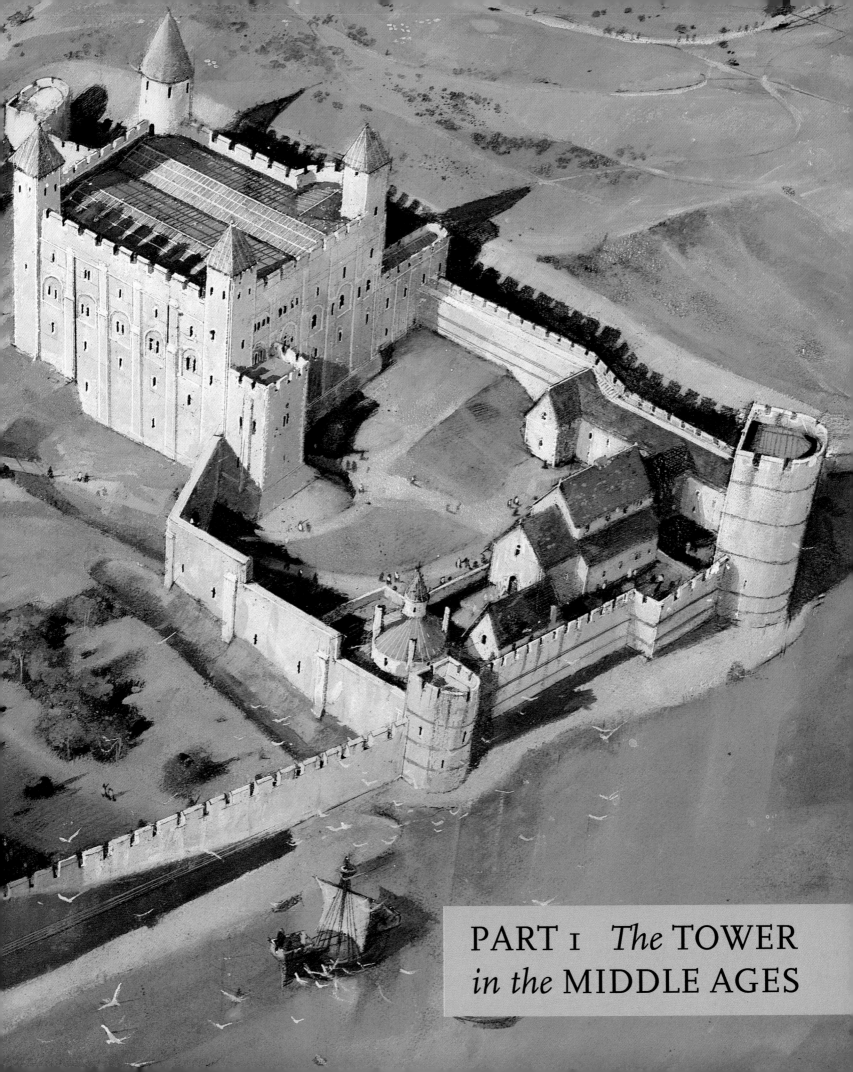

PART I *The* TOWER
in the MIDDLE AGES

BEFORE the TOWER AD 43–1066

Roman London and its walled defences create the site and setting for the future castle.

The Roman city

The history of the Tower of London begins in 1066, but the site was determined by buildings put up under the Romans, rulers of Britain from AD 43 to 410. Roman London as we know it probably began with the settlement of civilians in what is now the central area of the city, in about AD 50. The site was chosen because of its situation just above what was then the tidal limit of the River Thames, its well-drained position overlooking marshy ground, its accessibility from the Continent and easy communications inland. By then – on the eve of its destruction during Boadicea's revolt – it had become, according to the Roman historian Tacitus (c. AD 55–120), "packed with traders" and a celebrated centre of commerce. Ten years after the revolt the settlement had clearly recovered, and the first reference to it by name – as Londinium – dates from c. AD 70. The rebuilt city covered a large area, although it was not densely occupied. By about AD 80 it had a bridge – near the present London Bridge – and by the early second century a forum, a vast basilica (town hall), an amphitheatre, public baths and (to the north-west) a walled fort.

During the second half of the second century the future site of the Tower of London was built over, perhaps for the first time, as is shown by the foundations of Roman buildings revealed beside and even underneath William the Conqueror's White Tower. It was also in this century that some features of the city's modern street layout were first established, including, perhaps, the route of Great Tower Street, later to influence the siting of the castle's early entrances. But the known past of the Tower's site really begins in about AD 200, when the entire landward side of the city was enclosed by a massive defensive wall, over two miles long, part of which formed the castle's eastern rampart up to the 1240s, while most of the rest continued to protect the city until the seventeenth century. In about AD 250 a wall was also built along the riverside, probably in response to the new threat of seaborne attack by the Saxons, and in about AD 390 its eastern end, later also part of the Tower's defences, was partly rebuilt (figs. 2 and 3). The reinforcement of the river wall reflects the vigour of London's community, but also its

3. *View of the south-east corner of Roman London and the future site of the Tower of London as it might have looked in about AD 400, on the completion of the city wall along the river's edge. At the time of the Conquest, these defences still stood largely intact, and in 1066 provided William the Conqueror with an almost ready-made fortress. The White Tower was later built over the site of the domestic buildings shown at top left, but the rampart behind stood in some form until the 1240s. The foundations of the riverside towers may later have been re-used to carry new wall towers in the twelfth and thirteenth centuries.*

desperation. Roman-style city life may have lingered on for some time after the withdrawal of the Roman armies in AD 410, but the end was near.

Saxon London

Nearly seven hundred years elapsed between the collapse of Roman Britain and the Norman Conquest, but little is known about London's history and the Tower's site in this period. No single event is recorded between AD 457, when, according to a later source, the Britons of Kent, fleeing from rebellious Saxon settlers, took refuge within the city's walls, and the installation of a bishop, in 604. By then, London had a significant local populace, as it expelled the second bishop in 616, while its importance is shown by its possession of a mint in the eighth century and a contemporary reference to it as the capital of the

East Saxons and a centre of international trade. But the archaeological record, curiously, indicates that much of the walled city was then under cultivation, and that the main Saxon settlement was to the west of the Roman city, roughly on the site of the Strand. Nevertheless, there is evidence on and around the site of the Tower of London of the establishment of churches, and thus the origins of some landmarks that still exist today – the first being All Hallows by the Tower, probably towards the end of the seventh century (fig. 4). The city's resettlement, however, probably had to await the reign of King Alfred (871–899), who, according to his contemporary biographer, "restored London and made it habitable". Thereafter, two further churches appeared in the area: St Mary Magdalene by Aldgate, and probably St Peter ad Vincula, which was eventually enclosed within the castle.

4. *The Saxon archway (perhaps* C. AD 900*) that survives in All Hallows church, just to the west of the Tower. This and other churches in the area existed long before the Conquest, forming part of the urban landscape into which the castle was implanted.*

The CONQUEROR'S
Castle 1066–1100

The Tower is founded to control the city's "hostile inhabitants", and the White Tower, the gigantic stronghold that gave the place its name, is completed by 1100.

5. The south front of the White Tower in 1999. The main structure of the original building is very largely intact: as shown here, only the turret roofs (sixteenth century), the surrounds to the windows and doorways (eighteenth and nineteenth century) and a large part of the cut-stone dressings are not original. The timber staircase dates from 1973, but there must originally have been a similar one in the same place.

The Norman Conquest

The foundation of the Tower of London took place as a direct result of one of the most remarkable and important events in European history: the conquest, in 1066, of the rich and powerful kingdom of England by the Normans, rulers of a small state in central northern France. Their initial success was linked to their exceptional skills in war, inherited from their Viking ancestors, but their ability to conquer and hold the country can be attributed in part to their pioneering use of castles – of which the Tower of London was soon to become a supreme example.

The campaign of conquest was swift and effective. Once Duke William of Normandy had defeated the English army at Hastings (14 October 1066), he knew that he must secure London, the kingdom's richest and most populous city, but also that it might offer further resistance, so he avoided a direct attack. Instead, he isolated the city, marching north to cross the Thames at the town of Wallingford in Oxfordshire, where he received the submission of the Archbishop of Canterbury, before turning north-eastwards to Little Berkhamsted in Hertfordshire. The *Anglo-Saxon Chronicle*, an important contemporary history, tells us that "William was met there by ... all the chief men of London", that hostages were given, and that he in turn promised to be "a gracious liege Lord" to the English. His contemporary biographer, William of Poitiers, explains that he then "sent men ahead into London to build a fortress in the city" and to prepare

for his arrival. Although there may then have been further fighting at the city gates, William entered London a few days later, and was crowned on Christmas Day 1066 at Westminster Abbey. But aware of the "inconstancy of the numerous and hostile inhabitants", he then left London for Barking (Essex), "while fortifications were being completed". Whether the origins of the Tower of London lie in the first order or the second is not entirely clear, for, as he was later to do at York, he founded more than one castle. One of these, known by 1110 as Baynard's Castle, stood on the water's edge at the west end of the city (Blackfriars), just within the Roman wall; another, known by 1136 as Mountfichet's Castle, stood further north (in the area of Ludgate Circus), and was probably associated with the city's main west gate. Cryptic twelfth-century references to other fortifications – such as to the "little castle which was Ravengar's" in 1141 – suggest there may even have been others. The supremacy of the castle on the Tower's site, however, if not established from the start, was soon to be confirmed by the building of the White Tower.

The siting of the castle took advantage of the ready-made defences provided by the right-angle bend in the Roman city walls at their south-east corner, and made the city's strength immediately obvious to ships coming up river – factors that also ensured its continued predominance. William may also have been prompted by the exactly comparable position of the main fortress in Rouen, his capital in Normandy. The

In 1077 the *Anglo-Saxon Chronicle* records that much of London was destroyed by fire.

William Rufus scandalized his churchmen by removing night-lamps from his palaces: they took this as proof of his immoral life.

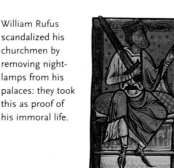

Bishop Flambard of Durham, the Tower's first known prisoner, escaped in 1100 by climbing through one of the White Tower's windows using a smuggled rope.

owners and inhabitants of the chosen site, like those whose houses were cleared away to build the castles at Oxford, Wallingford, Lincoln and elsewhere, can have had little say in its future.

Most castles built during the Conquest and the century after were of the 'motte and bailey' type (fig. 7), consisting of a mound, usually artificial, carrying a wooden tower or stockade, accompanied by an enclosure defended by a bank and ditch. Nevertheless, this arrangement seems not to have been used at the Tower site, where the ready-made defences provided by the Roman walls allowed the creation of an adequate fortress by enclosing the other two sides with a ditch (discovered by excavation in the 1960s) and an earthwork-and-timber rampart (fig. 13). The known enclosure must have contained the usual lodgings, storehouses, stables and other buildings. Given its small size, there may also have been an outer bailey, although no traces have survived. By 1086 the first Constable, Geoffrey de Mandeville, had been appointed to hold and manage the castle on the sovereign's behalf – the first of a succession of appointments since broken only in the sixteenth and seventeenth centuries.

The White Tower

The history of the castle as we know it today begins with the building of the White Tower, the gigantic structure at the centre of the complex that gave the Tower of London its name. The building's most striking feature is its immense size: at 36 x 32.5 m (118 x 106 ft) across and, on the south side (where the ground is lowest), 27.5 m (90 ft) tall, it is at least the second-largest structure of its type known to have been built. In addition, although endlessly altered in detail, the remarkable preservation of its general form makes it – if its purpose is correctly understood – the most complete eleventh-century palace in Europe.

The tower's two western corners are reinforced by square turrets, which rise above the battlements, the north-eastern corner by a round tower housing the main stair, and the south-eastern corner by the massive half-round projection housing the chapel apse. Inside, each of the building's four levels is divided into three main parts: a vast room takes up the whole of the west side, with a smaller one to the east, while the chapel and the spaces below it occupy the south-east corner. The lowest level, originally lit by small slits, half-underground and with no external entrance, was probably meant for storage only, although it contained access to the well – a vital feature if the tower was to resist a siege. The main entrance was to the floor above, originally reached from ground level by a timber staircase at the west end of the south wall (fig. 5). Both main rooms at entrance level were provided with fireplaces and the western one with latrines in the thickness of the wall (fig. 11). The floor above, reached by the spiral stair, is similarly equipped but had larger windows, while

9. Drain running, right to left, under the floor of the gallery in the thickness of the White Tower's wall, which carried water from the roof, originally at a lower level than today. It is composed of a split tree trunk lined with lead, and originally ended in a spout projecting from the west front.

10. *The south wall of the top-floor room on the east side of the White Tower, showing the soot stain that marks the position of the original roof at this level.*

tells us that Gundulf, Bishop of Rochester, and a known enthusiast for building, supervised "the king's works on the great tower of London ... for William the Great". As Gundulf was made Bishop in 1077, this has long been taken to show that it was begun, or even finished, in 1077–78. In fact, however, the text tells us only that Gundulf was involved after 1077 and before the King's death in 1087, so that work could have begun much sooner after the Conquest. In any case, new tree-ring dating shows that it was under way by 1081 – although structural and stylistic evidence implies an interruption during this decade – while references to the "tower" in 1097 and its use as a prison in 1100 for Ranulf Flambard, William Rufus's former chief minister, suggest that it had been completed by the end of the century.

both rooms open directly into the magnificent Chapel of St John the Evangelist (fig. 16). Above this there is now a further floor, but new discoveries have confirmed the long-held suspicion that this was not the original arrangement, and that the top floor was first inserted – along with the existing roof – in the late fifteenth century. The eaves of the original roof are now known to have been at the floor level of the existing top storey, and the roof-slopes to have been hidden and surrounded by the top stage of the Tower's walls (the mural gallery then being open to the weather on all sides). This arrangement is indicated by the outlines of pitched roofs in both existing top-floor rooms, and by the drains, recently discovered under the floors of the galleries, which must have carried rainwater from the roof. The traditional dating of the building has also been reconsidered. A text exists that

All this allows us to reconstruct the physical form of the original building, but questions remain as to why it should have been built in the form it was, what it was for, and where the ideas for its design came from. Written sources show that for well over one hundred years before the Conquest the kings and lords of France had been building towers in their main towns; although almost all have been destroyed, the superb example built in 1016–35 at Loches in Touraine (fig. 14) gives an idea of how impressive and sophisticated they could be. These demonstrated their owner's wealth and power – the medieval French term for such buildings, *donjon*, deriving from the Latin *dominium* (lordship) – but also functioned as residences and fortresses, or at least important parts of them. William's great grandfather, Duke Richard I (943–997), eager to show his equality with his rivals, put up towers in his main cities, Bayeux and Rouen,

RIGHT 11. *An original latrine built into the wall-thickness of the White Tower, one of the building's many sophisticated features and perhaps the earliest known example of such an arrangement in the country. Waste was discharged through an opening halfway up the building's outer wall.*

FAR RIGHT 12. *One of four wall fireplaces known to have existed in the White Tower. With the possible exception of those in the keep of the castle at Colchester (Essex), these are the earliest in England. The opening was originally spanned by a round arch, flush with the wall. The smoke escaped through small openings in the wall rather than through a true chimney.*

13. *The castle viewed from the south-west as it might have looked in the 1070s or 1080s, while the White Tower was in the early stages of construction. The small size of the Conqueror's earth-and-timber enclosure determined the siting of the new building, awkwardly close to the Roman wall.*

and it is hardly surprising that William should do so in the greatest city of his new kingdom.

Rivalled in London only by St Paul's Cathedral in scale and height until the nineteenth century, the White Tower was certainly well equipped to serve as a symbol of dominance. As a fortress it could have been equally effective – a stone building on this scale, with its entrance well above the ground, walls up to 4 m (13 ft) thick, would have been virtually impregnable in the eleventh century. But such a massive investment would not have been necessary if the building was not also to be a major peacetime residence, and this is clearly implied by the careful inclusion of fireplaces and latrines and the splendour of its chapel. Identifying the intended use of the other rooms within the White Tower, however, is another matter. Great medieval houses usually contained one particularly

large space for gatherings and smaller ones for the more private use of the occupant, generally referred to as the 'hall' and 'chambers' respectively. If the White Tower had contained a single residential floor, the vast western room could have been seen as the hall and its smaller neighbour the king's chamber. But the fact that it had *two* residential floors, with similar plans, raises some additional questions: were the first-floor rooms all part of the same house, or – as was frequently the case on the Continent in the twelfth century – was the top floor used by the most important occupants and the floor below by the rest? If the latter, it might be suggested that the grander upper floor was intended for the king's use, and the one below – with a chapel in the room below St John's – for the Constable. The exact truth may never be known.

Until recently there has been much debate about how such a sophisticated design could suddenly have been arrived at with no apparent precursors. But, as explained above, not only do we know that buildings of a generally similar size and type had long existed on the Continent, but it also now seems that the White Tower may have been fairly directly modelled on a particular building in Normandy dating from as early as AD 1000 – at Ivry-la-Bataille, near Evreux in Normandy (fig. 15). Although many more great keeps – such as those at Colchester, Castle Rising, Dover, Newcastle upon Tyne and Rochester – were built in the late eleventh and twelfth centuries, the White Tower remained, apart from Colchester, unsurpassed in size and reputation.

William the Conqueror died in 1087, and was succeeded as King of England by his second son, William Rufus (1087–1100), under whom the White Tower was completed. Rufus is also known to have made other alterations to the castle, although his greatest efforts were concentrated on rebuilding the royal palace at Westminster (of which the gigantic Great Hall, although much altered, is a survival): an entry in the *Anglo-Saxon Chronicle* for the year 1097 mentions "the wall they built about the tower" and the hardship caused by the conscription of the labour force. As this is the only reference to the work, exactly what Rufus achieved is unknown, but it may have seen the replacement of his father's timber rampart in stone, or, just possibly, the addition of a new enclosure to the north or west.

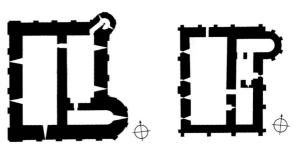

TOP 14. *The donjon or 'keep' at Loches (in Touraine, France), viewed from the north-east. Finished c. 1035, this clearly shows that defensible and residential towers on the scale of the White Tower had existed on the Continent well before the Norman Conquest.*

MIDDLE 15. *Reconstructed basement plans of the White Tower (left) and the tower at Ivry-la-Bataille in Normandy, of about AD 1000. The White Tower may have been modelled on Ivry, perhaps very directly.*

BOTTOM 16. *The interior of the Chapel of St John the Evangelist in the White Tower. Maintaining its eleventh-century form almost perfectly intact, this is one of the earliest and most exquisite Romanesque church interiors in the country. Its plan, complete with arcades and an aisle around all but one side, with a gallery above, reproduces an arrangement then typically found in the eastern ends of much larger churches.*

The TWELFTH CENTURY 1100–1200

The Norman castle's first expansion; a new moat and the building of the Bell Tower; palace buildings in the bailey.

17. The lower room in the Bell Tower, the most important twelfth- or early thirteenth-century interior in the castle.

The first major known expansion of the Conqueror's castle, and the creation of the earliest surviving buildings other than the White Tower, were undertaken in the twelfth century. The limited written evidence shows that William Rufus's younger brother and successor, Henry I (1100–1135), spent money on works at the Tower, possibly on the domestic buildings that Henry II (1154–1189) had to repair in the 1160s and 1170s. The 'pilaster' buttresses of the Wardrobe Tower, the ruins of which survive on the east side of the White Tower, suggest it, too, may be of this period.

The reign of Henry I's successor, his nephew Stephen (1135–1154), was overshadowed by struggles with a rival claimant, Henry's daughter Matilda. As Stephen's limited success was largely thanks to almost unbroken control of London, these years must have seen some activity, even if not much building work, at the Tower. Matilda's son Henry II, although among the greatest castle builders of the century, carried out no more than repairs – a testimony to the strength of the fortress he inherited. As it was a standard feature of his other keeps, he may nevertheless have been responsible for adding the protective turret or 'forebuilding' to the south side of the White Tower, demolished in 1674 but shown in a number of historic views (figs. 18, 55, 58 and 61). More is known, however, about activity towards the end of the century, when major works were undertaken for Henry II's eldest surviving son, Richard I

(1189–1199). Although a great founder (and probably designer) of castles in France and the Near East, Richard set out on the long-awaited Third Crusade in 1190 and spent only a few months in England during his entire reign. But it may have been on the King's orders – if not simply because the defences needed reinforcing – that his chief minister, William Longchamp, soon embarked on a major building programme at the Tower. The extent of what he did, or at least attempted, is indicated by the sums named in the surviving accounts – those of 1190, for example, adding up to twice as much as Henry II had spent on an entirely new castle at Orford (Suffolk) in the 1160s. Exactly what was carried out is not recorded. However, some indication of the nature of the work is suggested by archaeological evidence, the chronicles of Roger of Howden (a contemporary) and Matthew Paris (writing in the mid-thirteenth century), and surviving remains, although these might date from the reign of King John (1199–1216). Excavation has shown that a new ditch was dug parallel but to the north of the Conqueror's ditch (fig. 18), and on the same alignment. Together with the position of the magnificent Bell Tower (fig. 19), this allows an approximate reconstruction of the new bailey's size and shape. Attributable to the late twelfth or early thirteenth century on the basis of its unusual polygonal shape – found in similar towers of about 1200 at Dover, Corfe (Dorset) and Framlingham (Suffolk) – the Bell Tower also dates the south

LEFT The third Constable of the Tower, Othuer FitzEarl, died in the wreck of the *White Ship* along with Prince William, Henry I's son and heir.

RIGHT Thomas Becket was briefly Constable of the Tower in the 1150s before he was made Archbishop of Canterbury.

King Stephen tried to hold court at the Tower at Whitsun 1140, but his nobles and bishops were unwilling or afraid to join him there.

18. Reconstructed view of the castle from the south-west on the completion of the new defences, in about 1200. The White Tower then remained unaltered, except, probably, for the addition of the forebuilding to the south side. The bailey, however, had been extended westwards and reinforced by the massive Bell Tower, a new wall to the east of it, and a new western rampart, pierced by the main landward entrance at its far end. The buildings shown in the area immediately to the south of the White Tower (completely conjectural) represent the Great Hall and other residential buildings known to have existed by the 1160s.

curtain wall, which links it to the Wakefield Tower. The tower's junction with the existing (rebuilt) curtain wall to the north implies a contemporary rampart on the same alignment and thus implies a junction with the northern rampart on the site of the later Beauchamp Tower – perhaps also the site of the castle's main western entrance. Roger of Howden states that Longchamp also "caused the Tower of London to be surrounded by a moat of great depth", which, part new and part old, presumably ran right round the castle's landward side. Matthew Paris later claimed, with some satisfaction, that Longchamp's scheme to flood the moat from the river had failed.

Whether Longchamp actually completed all the works he intended is not certain, and expenditure in the next reign on wooden palisades suggests that there were still areas of weakness. But the scale of the Bell Tower and the fine, cut stonework of the contemporary wall give an idea of the quality of the work. When the castle was attacked by Richard's brother John in 1191, the new defences, even though incomplete, proved themselves effective – although Longchamp was forced to surrender for lack of supplies. In the following year the castle was further reinforced by palisades and stone-throwing engines, probably mounted on the main towers.

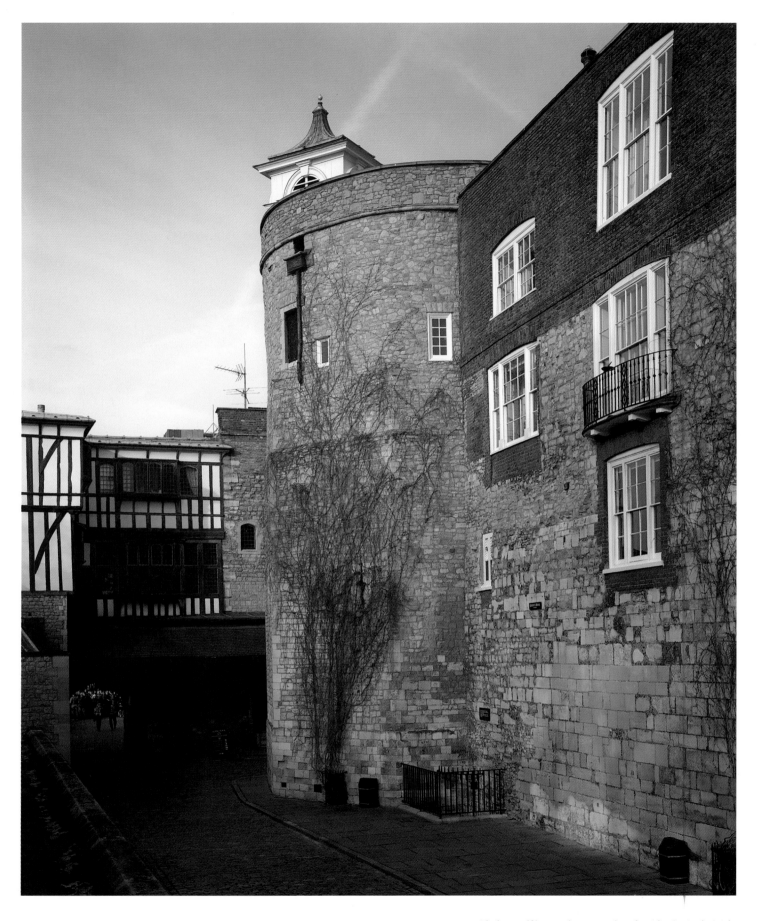

19. The late twelfth- or early thirteenth-century Bell Tower from the east, perhaps part of the new defences put up for Richard I. Originally rising sheer from the river's edge at the south-west corner of the castle, it was primarily defensive, but also contained accommodation.

23

The Castle
EXPANDS 1200–1307

Henry III's massive inner curtain wall and Edward I's outer wall and moat create one of Europe's greatest castles, and a layout that survives today.

The early thirteenth century

Although expenditure continued throughout the reign of King John, who succeeded his brother in 1197, no individual building within the Tower, destroyed or otherwise, can be attributed to him, although he made more personal use of the castle than almost any other monarch. All we know is that the accounts for 1214–15 record the building of a "mud wall" of unknown purpose "between the Tower and the City". Nevertheless, it may have been he who first established the Tower Menagerie – the collection of exotic animals that was to flourish there until 1835 (see pp. 29–30 and 101–05): certainly the earliest reference to this – the listing of an "allowance for the keepers of the lion and for the lion itself" – dates from his reign.

Henry III (1216–1272)

It was John's son, Henry III, and his grandson, Edward I (1272–1307), however, who created the basic form of the Tower as it is today. The situation that the nine-year-old Henry III inherited at his father's death in October 1216 could hardly have been worse, as much of the country was in the hands of the nobility (in revolt against King John). In London, the Tower, in rebels' hands since 1215, was by now the headquarters of their ally Prince Louis, heir to the French throne, whom they proposed to enthrone as the King of England: it was only after the Battle of Lincoln in May 1217 that the young

King's supporters defeated Prince Louis, re-established authority in Henry's name and regained the country's key fortress. Knowledge of these startling events can only have encouraged Henry, at least in later years, to appreciate the importance of fortifications and of his London base in particular.

In 1261 Londoners complained that the Constable of the Tower was impounding merchant ships on the Thames and selling their cargoes.

One of the Tower's most violent sieges took place in 1268 when the castle was successfully defended by the Jews of London and the Papal legate.

Edward I marked his victory over Llewelyn of Wales by mounting the Prince's head on the Tower's battlements, crowned with ivy.

Nevertheless, the first work to be done there, during the King's minority, was to the domestic buildings that had accumulated to the south of the White Tower in the area later known as the 'Inmost' or Palace Ward. Although we know that the 'King's houses', probably on this site, had been repaired by Henry II – and so may have existed since rather earlier – little is known about the buildings Henry III inherited. Nevertheless, it can be assumed that, like most major English houses of the Middle Ages, they incorporated a series of 'chambers' or private rooms and bedrooms grouped around a great hall – generally the largest room – which was used for ceremonies, as a court house and for formal dining.

The new work began in the 1220s with the construction of two towers incorporated in the riverside curtain wall – the Wakefield Tower and the Lanthorn Tower (rebuilt 1885–88), which reinforced the defences and provided extra accommodation. The only relics of Henry III's domestic buildings are the Wakefield Tower (fig. 23), jutting out into Water Lane from the southern curtain wall, as it once jutted out into the river, and the large gateway beside it – later incorporated in the Bloody Tower. The lower Wakefield chamber was intended as a guardroom or a storeroom, but the room above, equipped with large windows, a chapel, a fireplace and a possible bed-niche, may have been Henry III's principal bedroom (fig. 29). These remnants, together with the evidence of the King's written instructions for its fitting out, give a fairly good picture of its appearance in the 1220s and 1230s. To the east side of the Wakefield Tower, and linked to it via an intermediate chamber, was the Great Hall, which Henry substantially rebuilt. Recent research has shown that it measured as much as 24 m (80 ft) in length and 15 m (50 ft) wide, and was divided lengthwise into a central space and two side aisles (as in a church) by two timber arcades of four arches each. Other parts of the palace were also added to, altered and redecorated – sometimes more than once. Attention was also paid to the apartments given over to the Queen, Eleanor of Provence, which seem to have lain at the western end of the Great Hall, and some details of their decoration are recorded: the Queen's chamber, for example, was whitewashed and painted with flowers and false pointing to imitate cut stonework. Nevertheless, as he left it, the palace was probably less lavish and substantial than his other major residences at Clarendon (Wiltshire) and Winchester (Hampshire) – in keeping with his use of Westminster rather than the Tower as his usual London home.

In the late 1230s, however, the King's attention turned once again to the castle's defences, spurred on by renewed opposition to royal authority and a realization that they were, as the events of 1215–16 had proved, by now inadequate. Although not necessarily completed in Henry III's lifetime, the scheme he initiated saw a massive reinforcement of the Inmost Ward, in addition to the new Salt, Lanthorn and Wakefield towers on the south wall, and a huge expansion of the castle to the north and east. Henry also replaced the defences that had defined the

western edge of the Inmost Ward since the time of William Rufus or before with a massive stone-built wall, large parts of which survive, complete with a series of loopholes. The north end of the wall terminated in a massive twin-towered gatehouse (later called the Coldharbour Gate), built up against the side of the White Tower, which seems to have been finished by 1238. Although demolished in the 1670s, this is known from early drawings and its foundations, re-exposed to public view in the 1960s.

Henry's work to the buildings inside the Tower also ran to the maintenance and improvement of the White Tower, including the operation to which it owes its name: in March 1240 the King ordered a certain Richard de Freslingfield, Keeper of the Works at the Tower of London, "to have the Great Tower whitened both inside and out". This was followed in December by a second order to have the lead gutters of the Tower lengthened so that "the wall of the tower ... newly whitened, may be in no danger of perishing or falling outwards through the trickling of the rain" – indicating, perhaps, that it had not been whitewashed before. The reasons for the initial order are not given, but the King was no doubt prompted by the current European fashion for whitewashing great buildings, and by its dazzling effect. It must also have fooled many viewers, as it did two Irish travellers of the next century, into thinking that the rough masonry of the tower was in fact built (as they put it) "with immeasurable solidity from cut and dressed stone". A particularly enthusiastic builder and decorator of churches, Henry did not ignore the White Tower's chapel, ordering stained-glass windows and its decoration with paintings and statues. In addition, the Chapel of St Peter ad Vincula – by then enclosed within the castle – was almost entirely rebuilt.

By the time these operations were begun, Henry had already embarked on the greatest task of all – the refortification and enlargement of the castle itself. On the south side, still at the river's edge, the existing curtain wall was extended 50 m (160 ft) further east,

24. Interior of the first-floor room in the Salt Tower, built in about 1240. The tower had an important defensive role, but the fireplace, built-in latrine and the large west-facing window, originally overlooking the river, show that it was also meant to be lived in.

RIGHT 25. *Reconstructed view of the riverside defences of the Tower of London as left by Henry III, before the building of the Outer Ward in the 1270s. To the extreme left is the Bell Tower (c. 1200), and to the right the water-gate, which was later incorporated in the Bloody Tower. In the centre is the Wakefield Tower, to the right of which is the block of chambers that later served as the Record Office and was swept away only in the nineteenth century.*

BELOW 26. *Arrow slit in the lower floor of the Salt Tower, placed to allow an archer to shoot along the length of the curtain wall.*

beyond the line of the Roman wall, to a new tower, now called the Salt Tower. From this point the new wall ran due north, reinforced by three massive D-shaped towers – the Broad Arrow Tower, the Constable Tower and, at the north end, the Martin Tower, all opening on to the wall walk and provided with a stair to ground level. Vital to the defences, as they allowed archers to fire along the length of the wall's outer face from their tops and through arrow slits in their sides (fig. 26), the towers were also equipped with lodgings in their main upper rooms.

On the north side of the castle, the early ditch was filled in, the rampart demolished and a new one built running westwards from the Martin Tower. It, too, was reinforced by D-shaped towers – the Brick, Bowyer and Flint towers – larger and taller than the others so as to command the rising ground beyond. The landward defences, not protected by the river, were provided with a wet moat, excavated under the supervision of an engineer from Flanders, John 'le Fossur' (the ditcher), to ensure that this time it filled with water. Recent archaeological work suggests that he was highly successful: the moat was as much as 50 m (160 ft) across, and may have been provided with dams at the river's edge to keep the water in at low tide.

The castle's entrances on the river side – the postern leading up into the Wakefield Tower and the larger water-gate (later the Bloody Tower gate) – are well understood, but historians have long been puzzled as to the site of the main landward entrance in this period and before. This had been made all the more tantalizing by the chronicler Matthew Paris's detailed description of the demise of the entrance as rebuilt by Henry III: in the year 1240, he tells us, "on the evening of the Feast of St George [23 April], the stonework of a certain noble gateway which the king had constructed in the most opulent fashion collapsed, as if struck by an earthquake, together with its forebuildings and outworks". Paris goes on to say that the King then ordered the ruined gateway to be "rebuilt, more soundly this time and at still greater cost". But exactly a year later – as prophesied that night to a London priest by the ghost of Thomas Becket, patron saint of London – "the walls which had been built around the Tower collapsed irreparably". Other than that they faced the city, the situation of these doomed structures is not described. Archaeological excavations in 1995–97, however, revealed a massive and well-built stone platform (fig. 27), deep within the nineteenth-century fill of the existing moat, just west of the existing outer curtain wall and about 30 m (100 ft) north-west of the Beauchamp Tower. The thirteenth-century style of its masonry, the fact that it sloped at an alarming angle, and the dating of associated timbers driven into the ground behind it to 1240/41, leave little doubt that this was part of Henry's ill-fated defences. Exactly what part of them this particular building formed may never be known, but its position well forward of the main defences and the associated bridge suggest that it was an outer gateway – one of Paris's "outworks". In form, its lower part, containing the actual gate passage, was clearly square, but the shape of various fragments of stonework recovered from the surrounding fills, together with the existence of near-contemporary buildings of the same shape (for example at Dover and Kenilworth and at Trim and Carlinford in Ireland), suggest an elegant polygonal superstructure. The 'great gateway' itself must have been built into the curtain wall behind, and approached from the barbican by a narrow roadway (fig. 32).

The major setback of the 1240s necessarily slowed the process of refortification, such that even in 1253, when the King ordered the Constable to fortify "the whole breach of the bailey with a wooden stockade", the masonry defences remained incomplete. In 1261, however, the renewed crisis provoked by Henry's repudiation of an agreement in 1258 to give more power to the nobility (the Provisions of Oxford) led to an acceleration in the work. Exactly what was carried out is unknown, but large sums were spent on stone, timber, lime and lead, although even this left much to be finished in the next reign.

Not all Henry III's initiatives at the Tower, however, were confined to fortifications and domestic improvements. One of the more colourful was the expansion of the Menagerie, starting with the arrival in 1235 of three leopards, given by the Holy Roman Emperor Frederick II – a reference, perhaps, to Henry's coat of arms, which bore three such animals on a red background. In 1251 a white bear – perhaps a polar bear – was brought from Norway, and the Sheriffs of London were ordered to pay for his maintenance and to provide a muzzle, an iron chain and a cord long enough to allow him to fish in the Thames. Three years later Louis IX of France (1226–1270) presented its most spectacular occupant – an

27. *The base of a building discovered within the later fills of the western Tower moat in 1995. The style of the stonework and the date of the timber piles (foreground), established by dendrochronology, together with the skewed angle, almost certainly identify it as one of the forward defences that the thirteenth-century historian Matthew Paris tells us collapsed in 1240. The timber framing around the platform was joined to a timber bridge across the moat.*

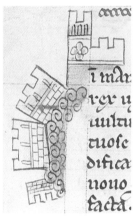

28. *Illustration drawn by Matthew Paris in the margin of an autograph copy of his* Greater Chronicle, *showing the collapse of Henry III's western defences in 1241, an event recently located and verified by archaeological excavation and scientific dating.*

elephant (fig. 33) – for which the King ordered a building measuring 12 x 6 m (40 x 20 ft) to be constructed, "in such a fashion and of such strength as to be fit for other uses when required". The King also paid attention to the Tower's surroundings, planting gardens, a vineyard and laying out a walled orchard to the north, the outline of which remained embedded in the area's topography until the 1950s.

Henry's reign also saw some important developments in the management of the royal finances and portable property which were to have far-reaching consequences for the Tower of London. In the twelfth and early thirteenth centuries this task had been supervised by a body called the Chamber – named after the king's private room, in which his money was frequently kept – and the management of household goods, weapons and valuables devolved to a subsidiary body, the Wardrobe (named from the French *garderobe*, literally a place of safekeeping for clothes). By the 1220s or 1230s, however, the Wardrobe had been established as an independent organization,

and had itself split into two parts – one responsible for perishable goods, particularly foodstuffs, and the other for everything else, including such diverse goods as furniture, jewels, weaponry, wax and spices. By the 1240s the Tower had become the main storehouse for the latter categories – the King himself being issued with a key to the main stores in 1249 – and by 1253 the stores and the body that managed them were being referred to as the Great Wardrobe. Thereafter, the activities of the Great Wardrobe, its offshoot the Privy Wardrobe, and the latter's descendants – the Armoury and the Board of Ordnance (see pp. 57–71 and 98–101) – were to play a key part in the functions and architectural development of the Tower until the nineteenth century.

Edward I (1272–1307)

Edward I was one of the most successful warrior-kings in English history and its best-known castle builder. On his return from a crusade in 1274, his attention turned to the Tower of London – presum-

29. Interior of the first-floor room in the Wakefield Tower. This room was possibly intended as the king's chamber. It was provided with a fireplace, while the wall to the left opens into a small chapel. A spiral stair led down to a private water-gate. Although the vault is a nineteenth-century reconstruction, and the chandelier and screen (based on medieval examples) were installed in 1993, the effect gives a good impression of the richness of a royal interior in the thirteenth century.

LEFT 30. *The Great Hall of Winchester Castle, completed for Henry III in 1235. Henry's Great Hall at the Tower was of a similar type, although slightly smaller. The exteriors of both were altered in a similar way in the fourteenth century.*

BELOW 31. *Remains of the rampart built by Henry III on the west side of the Inmost Ward, concealed by a succession of later buildings until re-exposed after bomb damage in the Second World War. Note the deep embrasures for arrow slits, designed to allow archers to fire through the wall as well as from the top.*

32. *Reconstruction of the Tower of London immediately before the collapse of 1241, showing Henry III's enlargement of the castle and the digging of the new moat in progress. The south-western corner of the earlier curtain wall has been retained, but the northern wall, built or extended in the previous century (fig. 18), has been demolished and is being replaced; a new rampart is also under construction to the east (right), extending the castle beyond the line of the Roman wall. The White Tower had been whitewashed in 1240, and the palace buildings in the Inmost Ward remodelled in the previous decade.*

ably part of his reassertion of royal authority after his own absence and the chaotic years under Henry III. At the Tower, he not only achieved the completion (although to a modified plan) of Henry's works, but also brought about the last major permanent transformation of the castle's layout. By the end of his reign all four sides of Henry's castle had been encircled by a new outer bailey (the Outer Ward) and a second curtain wall, enclosing ground reclaimed from the river on the southern side and surrounded on the others by a new moat. In doing so he created a 'concentric' castle, in which one wall encircles another – an obvious idea, and one used in the past, but which Edward I developed to a point of perfection.

As Henry III had been, Edward was obliged to compensate landowners over whose ground the castle was to be extended: St Katharine's Hospital,

for example, owner of the area to the east of the Tower, lost a mill and most of a garden, and was granted a perpetual annual income to make up for it. Heavy expenditure from May 1275 on wood and other materials to make tools for "the making the great ditch around the said Tower from the Thames towards the City to the Thames by St Katharine's hospital" suggests that site work began with the digging of the new moat. The first requirement was clearly to fill in the inner portions of the pre-existing moat to make ground for the new bailey, and this was supervised, once again, by a Fleming, Master Walter. Large-scale work continued until 1281, although wage payments had steadily decreased since 1276, suggesting that the bulk of the work had been achieved very quickly. As completed, the new moat was at least 50 m (160 ft) wide and many metres deep

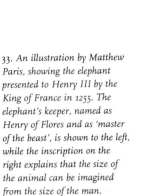

33. *An illustration by Matthew Paris, showing the elephant presented to Henry III by the King of France in 1255. The elephant's keeper, named as Henry of Flores and as 'master of the beast', is shown to the left, while the inscription on the right explains that the size of the animal can be imagined from the size of the man.*

at high tide. Although subsequently lined with a brick revetment (1670–83), drained and backfilled (1843–45), and encroached on by the Tower Bridge approach road (1886–94), this is the moat that surrounds the Tower today. Its main function was, of course, defensive – keeping assailants at a distance and protecting the new wall from undermining – but it had other uses, too, as a fishpond, a mill-pond and a convenient dumping ground for the castle's rubbish. In 1292 Edward I ordered a large number of young pike to be sent from Cambridge to stock the moat as a fishery, a function it retained throughout most of its history. The presence of mills at the Tower is known from a reference in an administrative document of 1276 to the felling of 600 beech trees in the King's Park at King's Langley (Hertfordshire) for "piles to be placed under the mill to the west of the Tower". A further 660 trees were felled

for an identical purpose for the "new mill towards St Katharine's" – in other words, on the east side of the castle. Exactly where the mills stood is not explained in the documents, but they are most likely to have stood on the dams across the moat at its two junctions with the river, where they could have been powered by the water trapped in the moat at high tide. This was supported by the discovery during excavations in 1996 of tree trunks driven into the river bed under both dams, which had been cut down in 1276, the year the mills were built. Although the dams and the causeways they carried survived, the mills themselves disappeared quite soon: possibly in restricting the outflow of water, they speeded up the silting of the moat – clearly a serious problem from the beginning, as an order was issued for dredging it as early as 1293.

The inner edge of the moat was lined with a wall, set out more or less parallel to the earlier curtain, leaving a gap of up to 30 m (100 ft) between the two ramparts. To make this reclaimed ground useable, the sloping bank that had risen up to the foot of Henry's walls was cut away, leaving the original postern gate to the south of the Broad Arrow Tower well above ground level (fig. 37). The wall itself, on the landward sides, seems at first to have been no more than a revetment and parapet – owing partly, perhaps, to the instability of the newly reclaimed ground and to cost, but also to allow archers to fire at an enemy from both inner and outer ramparts. Similar arrangements were made at several of Edward's Welsh castles – Aberystwyth and Rhuddlan (begun 1277), Harlech (begun 1283) and Beaumaris (begun 1295) – and the Clare family's great

34. *Edward I and his Queen, Eleanor of Castile, adorning the letter 'A' in a fourteenth-century chronicle of the King's life. Edward made relatively little use of the Tower himself, but was responsible for extending it to its present size and creating the existing moat.*

35. *Exit chutes for a series of latrines built into Brass Mount, the broad, round bastion placed by Edward I at the north-east corner of his new outer curtain wall, overlooking the moat.*

Latrines emptying directly into the moat continued to be used at the Tower until the 1840s, but the resulting pollution contributed to the eventual decision to fill it in.

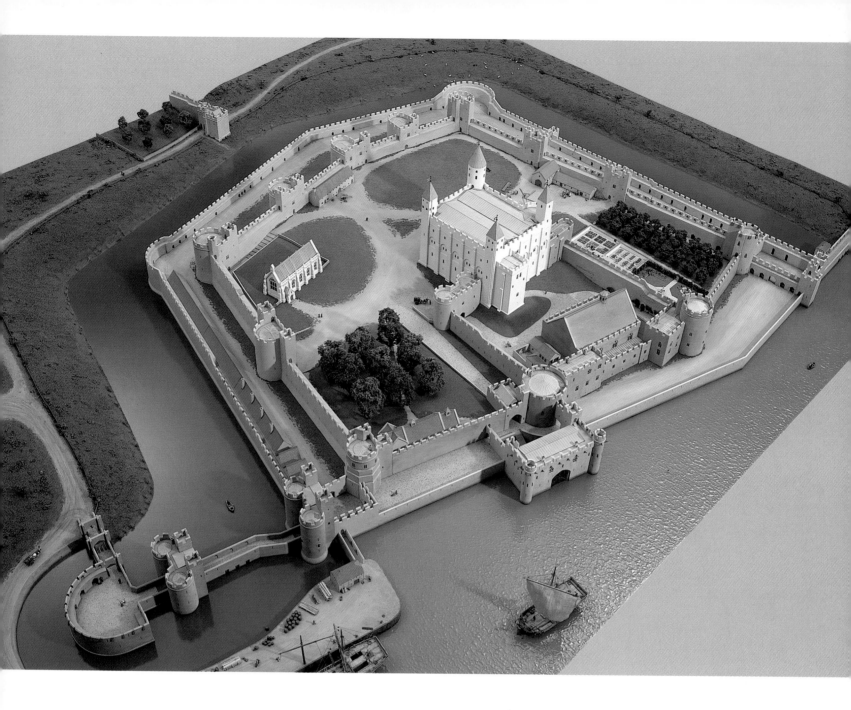

36. Model of the Tower of London as it might have looked on the completion of the works planned by Edward I (c. 1300). Edward's improvements had included the creation of the existing moat, the outer curtain wall along its inner edge, the elaborate outer defences of the western entrance (lower left), and St Thomas's Tower, projecting into the river. The essentials of the layout are the same today, although the Lion Tower and its moat have largely disappeared and the wharf, here extending westwards only as far as the Byward Tower, had been extended all the way along the south side by about 1400, creating the south moat.

stronghold at Caerphilly (begun 1268). As also at Harlech and Caerphilly, potential for extra firepower was provided by broad, rounded projections at the rampart's northern corners (Legge's Mount and Brass Mount), at first no higher than the walls on either side. Later in Edward's reign, or early in the next, both walls and bastions were heightened, while towards the north end of the east curtain wall, two curious square projections (see plan inside front flap) – perhaps intended to carry stone-throwing engines – were added, propped by sloping bases extending far out into the moat.

The extension of the castle on the south side meant building out into the river, presumably achieved by driving piles into the river bed and backfilling with earth and rubble. In this case the wall was, from the first, more than just a parapet, although this, too,

was later heightened. The newly enclosed area – the southern arm of the outer bailey – is now called Water Lane. An effect of this, of course, was to leave the earlier wall and Henry's main water-gate – the Bloody Tower – and the nearby Wakefield postern high and dry, making it necessary to create a new riverside gate, which took the form of St Thomas's Tower (see fig. 40; see also p. 38). Between 1275 and 1281 Edward also reorganized the landward approaches, moving the main gate to the south-west corner of the castle and protecting it with a complex series of outworks (fig. 36). When completed, the route into the castle from Tower Hill passed first of all across a stone causeway to a massive semicircular enclosure (the Lion Tower), surrounded by an extension of the main moat and defended by two gates and a drawbridge. Beyond that, the visitor was con-

34

RIGHT 37. *The postern gate in the inner curtain wall on the east side of the castle, built in about 1240, and originally opening on to a bank sloping down to the moat. The clumsy thickening of the wall below dates from the 1270s, when the bank was cleared away to make more room between the old wall and the new.*

ABOVE 38. *Aerial view of the castle at Harlech (Gwynedd), one of a series of strongholds built in the 1280s by Edward I to secure his conquest of the Principality of Wales. Here, as had already been achieved at the Tower, Rhuddlan (Clwyd) and Caerphilly (Glamorgan), and was soon to be the case at Beaumaris (Anglesey), the defences were arranged concentrically, the more modest outer rampart providing a first line of defence and useful extra space within the fortified area.*

RIGHT 39. *Brass Mount, part of Edward I's outer curtain wall, showing the horizontal break (about one third of the way up) between the original work of the 1270s and the heightening of c. 1300.*

fronted by a twin-towered gatehouse (the Middle Tower), housing a passageway defended by a drawbridge, a massive gate and two portcullises. From there, a parapeted causeway led across the moat to a second, larger twin-towered gatehouse (the Byward Tower), again defended by a drawbridge, gate and portcullises; beyond this, inside the castle, were further gateways to the western and southern arms of the new Outer Ward. A substantial part of the complex survives, including the two gatehouses, the causeway between them (fig. 41) and part of the causeway from the Lion Tower to Tower Hill, re-exposed in the 1930s. But the most remarkable part of the complex, now almost completely destroyed, was the Lion Tower – so called because, from at least the 1330s, it housed the lions of the king's Menagerie. Surrounded by its own moat and a battlemented parapet (fig. 36), this provided a 180-degree field of fire for a large number of archers, ideal for scattering an attacking force at its first approach. Although a 'half-moon' bastion is to be found at Goodrich (Herefordshire) of *c.* 1300, this is England's earliest surviving example, perhaps based on those Edward I had seen in France, and which he may himself have built there

at his frontier towns. Similar bastions were later widely used both to carry and to resist artillery.

The final major operation was the building (or rebuilding) of the western inner curtain wall, which, although faced in stone, was mostly built of brick (243,000 were ordered in 1276–78), one of the first large-scale uses of this material in England since Roman times. The last stage was the building of the gigantic Beauchamp Tower between June and December 1281. This was begun only when the gateway it replaced – perhaps never properly rebuilt after 1240 – had been superseded by the completion of the new western entrance. Outside the Tower, the south end of the newly truncated city wall was provided with a new tower and postern gate on the moat's edge (fig. 44).

Although Edward I concentrated on the Tower's defences, he also improved its accommodation. Beyond the Wakefield Tower, formerly the king's innermost room, Edward created further residential quarters over the new water-gate (St Thomas's Tower), linked to the Wakefield Tower by a first-floor bridge (rebuilt in the nineteenth century) across the newly created Outer Ward (Water Lane). This remark-

able building took the form of a massive rectangular block, projecting into the river from the riverside curtain wall. The lower level was largely taken up by a water-filled basin, linked to the river by the actual water-gate (closed with a portcullis) and spanned at the rear by a gigantic archway, allowing small boats to dock inside the castle. The upper floor contained two rooms, described in an administrative document of 1276–77 as "containing a hall with a chamber above the gate over the water of the Thames river". Equipped with a tiny oratory, fireplaces and latrines, it may have been meant to provide King Edward with a private suite of rooms. The protection of the river allowed and invited the decoration of the outside, and the accounts and later images show that it had wide, stained-glass windows looking out over the water and was decorated with painted statues. In general form, although remarkable for its riverside location, St Thomas's Tower has much in common with the great residential gateways that the King built at Harlech and Beaumaris, and that the Clares built at Tonbridge and Caerphilly in the 1260s.

As his father had done, Edward also turned his attention to the Chapel of St Peter ad Vincula, which

43. The Beauchamp Tower of 1281, viewed from the west. Deliberately intended to provide an impressive sight from the city, the tower was built on or near the site of the 'noble gateway', which had collapsed in 1240.

44. *Model of the postern tower and gate, viewed from the west (outside the city), attached to the end of the Roman and medieval city wall at the point where it met Edward I's moat.*

was, it seems, rebuilt again, although all except its north wall was later swept away by Henry VIII.

Edward I's reign also saw the permanent establishment at the Tower of a major branch of the Royal Mint, another institution that was to play a large part in the castle's history until the nineteenth century. By the 1270s the English coinage, last entirely recalled and re-minted in 1248, was worn out and further damaged by years of deliberate 'clipping'. In November 1278 suspicion of particular guilt fell on a number of financiers, mostly Jewish, and large numbers were arrested throughout the kingdom and some imprisoned at the Tower. Further arrests followed, and in 1279 a number of goldsmiths and financiers were executed for crimes relating to the debasement of or damage to coinage. How many of these individuals were actually guilty is, of course, unknown, but the scandal emphasized the need for greater security and control of the London Mint,

which, although only one of several mints, was the most important. Documents record a flurry of building activity almost certainly associated with the Mint, including expenditure on "the little tower where the treasure of the mint is kept". Where these buildings were is uncertain, but the 121 m (400 ft) long building put up to house thirty new furnaces must have been housed in the Outer Ward, and probably in its western arm, the present Mint Street. The heightening of the outer curtain wall was probably undertaken to protect the new buildings.

This period also saw the consolidation of the Tower as the Great Wardrobe's main repository for arms and armour, managed and augmented by the workshops present there since at least 1273. In addition, after an attempted theft in 1303 at Westminster (the Great Wardrobe's other principal place of storage), the more valuable and precious-metal items that it had looked after were transferred to the Tower.

The LATER MIDDLE AGES 1307–1485

The Tower plays its part in the Hundred Years' War,
the Peasants' Revolt and the Wars of the Roses,
and is expanded for the last time.

LEFT 45. *View through the
Bloody Tower gate passage
showing the highly decorative
vault inserted for Edward III
between 1360 and 1362 by
Robert Yevele, brother of Henry,
one of the most famous
architects of the Middle Ages.
From an engraving by Frederick
Nash, 1821.*

RIGHT 46. *Edward III
disembarking at Le Largue in
1345. Military and personal
supplies of the kind being
unloaded around the King were
stored at the Tower of London
and loaded at the Tower wharf.*

Edward II (1307–1327)

The reign of Edward I's son, Edward II, saw relatively little activity at the Tower, although he used it on occasion as a residence and a refuge. Certainly he needed it, for, disastrously lacking in military skill or statesmanship, by 1311 he had plunged the country into a two-year civil war, largely owing to the nobility's hatred of his favourite, Piers Gaveston; a second war in 1326–37, provoked by another favourite, Hugh Despenser, was to cost him the throne and his life. Nevertheless, apart from the reconstruction of the riverside wall between the Byward Tower and St Thomas's in 1324, the fabric of the Tower was largely neglected. Edward's reign did, however, see significant growth in the importance of some of the functions and institutions that were to dominate the castle in later centuries (see Part 2), among which was its role as a place for safeguarding important state and legal records. Although this had been the case since the earliest years, by the 1320s record storage had already expanded into the White Tower chapel – beginning a long process of usurping former royal accommodation – while in the same decade, again anticipating the practice of later centuries, the records were systematically sorted and filed under location.

Edward III (1327–1377) and the Hundred Years' War

Under Edward II's son, Edward III, the castle was once again substantially altered, partly owing to the

consolidation of another role it was to enjoy for many centuries – as a vital centre for the supply and storage of military equipment. The new King's attention turned to the castle in 1335, when he ordered a survey of its condition and an estimate for its repair to be drawn up. Prominent among the resulting works were further improvements to Edward I's defences, particularly the heightening and crenellation of the eastern arm of the south curtain, between 1336 and

In 1336 Edward III ordered the Tower's gates to be locked from sunset to dawn and forbade the officers and guards to stay out in the city at night.

LEFT Henry IV created the Order of the Bath in 1399. By custom, a knight bathed in the White Tower as part of his initiation.

RIGHT George, Duke of Clarence, was executed in 1478 by drowning in a butt of Madeira. Legend places his dungeon in the Bowyer Tower.

extending the small quay that had adjoined the Lion Tower in the previous century had begun in the 1330s, the eastward extension as far as St Thomas's Tower took place in 1338, and was followed by further extensions in 1360 and 1369. Another immediate result of the war was an increasing demand for space to store military supplies. This was frequently answered at the expense of formerly domestic accommodation, even of the highest status: by 1336, for example, Edward I's rooms in St Thomas's Tower were being used for storing crossbows and armour. In addition, however, Edward III may also have created new storage facilities in the form of the very substantial building once attached to the east side of the White Tower, now lost, but known in some detail from early plans and drawings (figs. 55 and 88; see also fig. 66). The pressures of war were also affecting the way in which the Tower's stores were managed, and by 1361 the headquarters of the Great Wardrobe had moved to new premises near Baynard's Castle, and a new subsection, the Privy Wardrobe, was established at the Tower under its own keeper and given responsibility for military supplies. These competed for space with the Privy Wardrobe's other responsibility for the king's jewels and coronation equipment (other than sacred items, kept at Westminster Abbey): an inventory of 1357 of the "treasury in the high tower of London", which lists, among much else, a "pair of spurs for the King's coronation", a bishop's crozier, a gilded silver crown and five sceptres, gives an idea of its richness and variety.

Another result of the war was that, although he rarely used the Tower himself, Edward's victorious campaigns gave it a renewed importance as a state prison: from 1346 to 1357 it housed Edward's brother-in-law, King David Bruce of Scotland, captured at the Battle of Neville's Cross, and in 1360 the King of France, Jean II (Jean le Bon, 1350–1364), captured at Poitiers in 1356. The French King was provided with apartments in the White Tower, emptied of stored records and reorganized for his use, and in which he and his entourage lived in some style until his release a few months later.

1340, and the construction of a small water-gate – the Cradle Tower – in the late 1340s and early 1350s towards its eastern end. An elegant creation with an upper storey (rebuilt in the nineteenth century) over a single gate passage, with guard rooms to either side, it probably provided private access to the royal lodgings. At the extreme south-east corner of the castle, the Develin Tower and a new causeway were constructed to allow at least pedestrian access via a single gate and a causeway to St Katharine's Hospital, perhaps replacing a similar arrangement dating from the 1270s.

Within the castle, detailed accounts show that the Great Hall was substantially altered in 1336–37, with the replacement of the now-outmoded gables that had framed its north windows by a flat parapet – precisely as was to happen to the surviving Great Hall at Winchester Castle (fig. 30) under Richard II (1377–1399). Later in the reign, the Constable's lodgings were rebuilt, probably on the site of the largely sixteenth-century Queen's House – now used by the Tower's Resident Governor (fig. 159) – which certainly contains fabric of this period. Less ambitious improvements included the extension of Henry III's water-gate beside the Wakefield Tower to form the basis of the existing Bloody Tower, and the creation of the beautiful vault over the gate passage (fig. 45).

Much of the remaining activity and developments at the Tower of London under Edward III were closely associated with the Hundred Years' War, an intermittent conflict between France and England that began with the King's claim to the French throne in 1340 and ended with a final French victory in 1453. The most important and enduring physical change that it engendered was the building of the Tower wharf, in direct response to the demands of supplying English forces abroad: although work on

Richard II (1377–1399)

In the later part of the fourteenth century the Tower was closely associated with the rise and fall of Edward III's unfortunate successor, his grandson Richard II, son of the Black Prince. The reign began with the King's stay at the Tower before his coronation, and a dazzling procession from the castle to Westminster Abbey, following a tradition dating from at least as early as 1308 and that was to last until 1660 (see pp. 52–55). But the reign also ended there. In 1399 the King's first cousin, John of Gaunt's son, Henry of Bolingbroke, exiled and deprived of his vast inheritance, invaded the country in Richard's absence and

48. *Richard II surrenders the regalia to his cousin Henry Bolingbroke, as depicted in a fifteenth-century copy of Jean Froissart's* Chronicles *of c. 1460–80. The event took place at the Tower in September 1399.*

49. *Richard II confronts the mob at Mile End, as shown in a fifteenth-century copy of Jean Froissart's* Chronicles. *The scene to the left shows Wat Tyler being struck down by the Mayor of London while the King looks on; to the right, Richard is shown exhorting the rebels to accept him as their leader in Tyler's place and to disperse.*

was crowned king within six months. Captured and imprisoned in the Tower, Richard was forced to abdicate there – perhaps, as tradition has it, in the White Tower. A year later he died, probably of starvation, in Pontefract Castle (Yorkshire).

The Tower was also closely involved in one of the major events of the reign – the Peasants' Revolt of 1381. The vast cost of the war with France – renewed in 1369 and by then going badly – led to the attempted imposition (for the third time since 1377), of a 'poll' tax, levied on everyone over the age of fourteen. This led to widespread protest, culminating in the march on London in June 1381 of hordes of peasants – said by contemporaries to number up to 20,000 – under Wat Tyler, Jack Straw and John Ball. Admitted to the city by sympathisers within, they set about sacking buildings associated with the King's 'evil councillors', including John of Gaunt's magnificent suburban palace, the Savoy (today the site of the Savoy Hotel). Richard II, meanwhile, accompanied by his mother, two half-brothers, other lords and clerics and his unpopular Chancellor and Archbishop of Canterbury, Simon of Sudbury, had taken refuge in the Tower. With the rebels camped all round them the King agreed to meet their leaders the next day at Mile End, and there, following the killing of Wat Tyler by the Mayor of London (fig. 49) and the young King's courageous defusion of the resulting crisis, the mob dispersed. Before then, however, one of the stranger events in the Tower's history had taken place: its capture, in spite of its status as one of Europe's strongest castles, by an ill-armed mob. As the contemporary author Jean Froissart relates in his *Chronicles*, as soon as the gates had been opened to let the King out, four hundred rebels rushed in, headed for the innermost parts of the castle, and ransacked the King's apartments. The rebels "arrogantly lay and sat and joked on the king's bed, whilst several asked the king's mother … to kiss them"; she was carried to safety by river but the unfortunate Sudbury was dragged out with a number of other victims and butchered on Tower Hill (fig. 50).

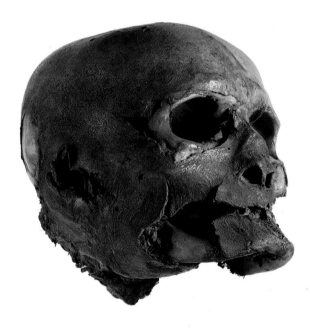

ABOVE 50. *The head of Simon Sudbury, Archbishop of Canterbury, murdered on Tower Hill during the Peasants' Revolt in 1381.*

RIGHT 51. *Detail of a wall painting in the Byward Tower, rediscovered in a fragmentary condition in 1953. Representing either the Crucifixion or the Last Judgement, the style of the painting and details of its content suggest it dates from the reign of Richard II (1377–1399).*

52. *Embrasure inside the turret attached to the south side of the Byward Tower in the late fifteenth century, designed for the deployment of small cannon. This is the earliest adaptation for defence by firearms to survive at the Tower of London.*

Later in the reign, the Tower was once again involved in a major crisis, when, in 1387, following a failed attempt to reassert authority over his rebellious ministers, the King was forced to change his plans and spend Christmas at the Tower rather than at Windsor. The hasty preparations made for his arrival, including the "removal of the stones for the cannons and the carriage of two springalds [catapults] from the Lord King's Great Hall in the said Tower", illustrate very poignantly the relative importance of the Tower as a refuge rather than as a normal residence.

The end of the reign saw the final eastward extension of the wharf under the direction of the Clerk of Works – the poet Geoffrey Chaucer, no less – reaching the far shore of the east moat by 1389. This had the obvious result of creating the south moat, and sealed off the newly built Cradle Tower from the river, although St Thomas's Tower was kept accessible through a bridged opening in the wharf.

The fifteenth century

Although there was relatively little building work at the Tower in the fifteenth century, the castle played a significant part in the events and politics of the period. At the very beginning of the reign, for example, it provided the refuge that allowed Henry IV (1399–1413) to survive an attempted *coup d'état* by the late King Richard's supporters. It also served, as under Edward III, as a prison for many illustrious victims of the King's campaigns – beginning with the conspirators of 1400. In 1406 the young heir to the throne of Scotland (soon to be James I of Scotland) was seized quite illegally on the way to France, and began a long imprisonment at the Tower; he was followed, in 1408, by the son and family of Owen Glendower, the Welsh patriot whom Henry had finally defeated in that year. Henry V (1413–1422), who succeeded in 1413, took the country into a new phase of the Hundred Years' War, and his victory at Agincourt in 1415 and later campaigns filled the castle with new batches of important prisoners, including the French King's nephew Charles, Duke of Orléans, held there intermittently from 1415 until 1440 (fig. 56). The rise of the Lollards in this period (who shared some of the beliefs held by the Protestants of the next century) also led for the first time to the incarceration of individuals not only on political but also on religious grounds – foreshadowing the regular practice of the Tudor and Stuart periods. The first and most celebrated victim was the Lollard and rebel Sir John Oldcastle, taken from the Tower and executed in 1417.

In the second half of the fifteenth century the Tower was inevitably caught up in the struggle between the descendants of Edward III's sons, Edmund Duke of York (Yorkists) and John of Gaunt, Duke of Lancaster (Lancastrians) – later called the Wars of the Roses. The castle first saw action in 1460, when it was held for Henry VI (1422–1471) against the supporters of his opponent, Richard Duke of York, by whom the King had been captured at Northampton in July of that year. A contemporary tells us that the Tower's commander, Lord Scales, aware of this, threatened by the Londoners and now clearly desperate, "cast wild fire into the city, and shot in small guns ... and hurt men and women and children in the streets", while the citizens "laid great bombards [cannon] on the far side of the Thames ... and crazed the walls thereof in divers places". How much damage was really done is unknown, but on 19 July, with no hope of relief, Scales surrendered. The brief revival of Henry's cause after the Lancastrian victory at Wakefield (December 1460) was crushed by Richard of York's son, Edward, at Towton (March 1461), forcing Henry into hiding and allowing York to claim the throne as Edward IV (1461–1483). Recaptured in 1465, Henry was brought "as a traitor and criminal to London, and imprisoned in the Tower there; where, like a true follower of Christ, he patiently endured hunger, thirst, mockings, derisions, abuse and many other hardships". He was held until briefly reinstated during Edward's temporary overthrow in September, but this was ended by Edward's

victorious return in March 1471, which led to a hasty reinforcement of the Tower, particularly along the wharf, where earthworks were thrown up and gun emplacements improvised with earth-filled barrels. Although this successfully resisted a ship-borne bombardment, and land forces were driven off by a sortie, the real issue was decided by the battles of Barnet and Tewkesbury, and in May 1471 Edward IV re-entered London in triumph. Henry's fate is the stuff of legend: while his former opponents held that he had died of grief, his supporters rightly claimed he had been murdered. A contemporary claimed that he had been "stykked with a dagger by the hands of Edward's brother the Duke of Gloucester" (the future Richard III), an event that tradition, although probably incorrectly, places in the Wakefield Tower (fig. 29).

The final years of Edward IV's reign saw the last extension of the Tower's fortified area with the creation of an enclosure at the south end of Tower Hill to protect the western entrance, the first of the Tower's defences designed to carry and resist gunfire; early views and excavation show that it was built of brick and may have been protected by a moat; if so, the Tower dock (an inlet from the river that survived until 1953) may have been its last remnant. The outpost's safety was entrusted to a new official, Thomas Redhede, appointed to the office of Porter of the Tower of London and Keeper of 'le Bulwark', as it became known, in March 1484. He was provided with a house inside it, and later made a profitable, if illegal, business of subletting houses to his neighbours. Either in this reign or later in the century the security of the postern gate on the south side of the Byward Tower was improved with the building of the existing triangular-shaped turret, equipped with loopholes for small cannon and handguns – an early and important example of such an arrangement (fig. 52).

Edward IV's death in 1483 was followed by one of the most famous (and also one of the most unpleasant) events in the Tower's history: the murder of the 'Princes in the Tower'. Within a month of Edward V's accession, the dead King's brother, Richard Duke of Gloucester, had proclaimed himself Protector and confined the twelve-year-old Prince in the Tower. Overcoming opposition from the Prince's supporters – notably Lord Hastings, who was arrested at a council meeting in the castle and summarily murdered – Gloucester then proclaimed himself Richard III, and was crowned in July 1483. The fate of Prince Edward and his younger brother, Richard, who had later joined him at the Tower, is well established, even if the details are unclear: they were last seen alive in June 1483, and during the autumn were quietly murdered. Their bodies were hidden, but in 1674, during the demolition of the twelfth-century

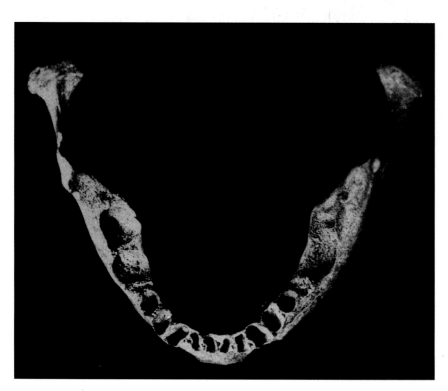

53. *The lower jaw of one of the two skeletons unearthed at the Tower in 1674, identified as those of Edward V and his brother Richard and redeposited in Westminster Abbey. Re-examination in 1933 showed them to be of two boys, one aged about ten and the other about twelve, making this identification entirely plausible.*

forebuilding on the south side of the White Tower (see p. 62), the "bones of two striplings" were discovered, identified as those of the young princes, and placed in an urn in Westminster Abbey. Not diminished by this event, opposition to Richard III grew rapidly from the beginning of his reign. It culminated in his defeat in 1489 at the Battle of Bosworth (Leicestershire) by Henry Tudor, a descendant of Edward III, who took the throne as Henry VII, founder of the dynasty that ruled the country for the whole of the following century.

Political events and its role as a fortress and prison apart, the fifteenth century saw the continued development of the Mint, the Record Office, the Wardrobe, the Jewel House and the Menagerie – all of which have been mentioned above and are discussed in more detail in Part 2. But among the other organizations and institutions that were to mould or feature prominently in the castle's later history, three – the Yeoman Warders, the Armoury Office, and the Office of Ordnance (see below) – trace their origins to the fifteenth century. The precise date at which the

Yeomen of the Guard – the royal bodyguard of which the Yeoman Warders were a detachment – formed is unknown, but they were well established by 1509, and almost certainly originated in the reign of Edward IV, Richard III or Henry VII. The Armoury, together with the Ordnance, emerged as a successor body to the Privy Wardrobe, which had assumed responsibility for the king's weapons and precious items in the 1250s (see p. 30). In the first decade of the fifteenth century the Keeper of the Privy Wardrobe ceased to appear in the accounts, and some of his functions were assumed by the 'Keeper of the King's Armour in the Tower', establishing an organization that survived, with its own staff and with designated premises at the Tower, until the seventeenth century. The origins of the Ordnance as an independent body probably date to the appointment in 1414 of a certain Nicholas Merbury as 'Master of the Kings engines and guns and of the Ordnance', and its influence steadily increased, in line with the importance and sophistication of artillery, as the century progressed.

55. Combined plan and 'bird's-eye' view of the Tower of London prepared (probably in 1597) to accompany a report on its condition. The version shown here is a copy of the original (now lost) made for the Society of Antiquaries of London, and from which the better-known engraving was taken in 1742. Not only is this the earliest measured plan of the Tower, and full of meticulous detail, but it also shows the castle at a time when many of its medieval and Tudor buildings, swept away or drastically modified in the seventeenth century, were still largely intact. Note in particular the thirteenth-century defences of the western entrance, the vast Ordnance storehouse and offices of 1545–47 (to the north), the royal lodgings and 'The Hall decay'd', and the cannon on the roof of the White Tower, placed there in 1534. Thanks probably to the plan's use in settling a dispute over the status of the Tower Liberties (the area around the Tower and under its control), it also shows their boundary and much topographical detail within it.

Lord *Lumley's* House sometime belonging to *Crutched Fryers*

The New Brick Wall

Pike's Garden

TOWER HILL

The Posts of the Scaffold

Barkin Church

TOWER STREET

The Houses betwixt the Church Yard and the Hill are St Katherines Rents.

THAMES STREET

Petty Wales

The Bulwark Gate

The Lyons Gate

The Lyons Tower

The Lieutenants Lodging

SEMPER EADEM

The DESCRIPTION of the TOWER of LONDON with all the Buildings and the Outermost Limits thereof together with all such places adjoyning as do confine and abound the said Liberties. made by the direction of Sr John Peyton Knt.

SCALA PERTICARUM.

PART 2 *The* TOWER *and its* INSTITUTIONS

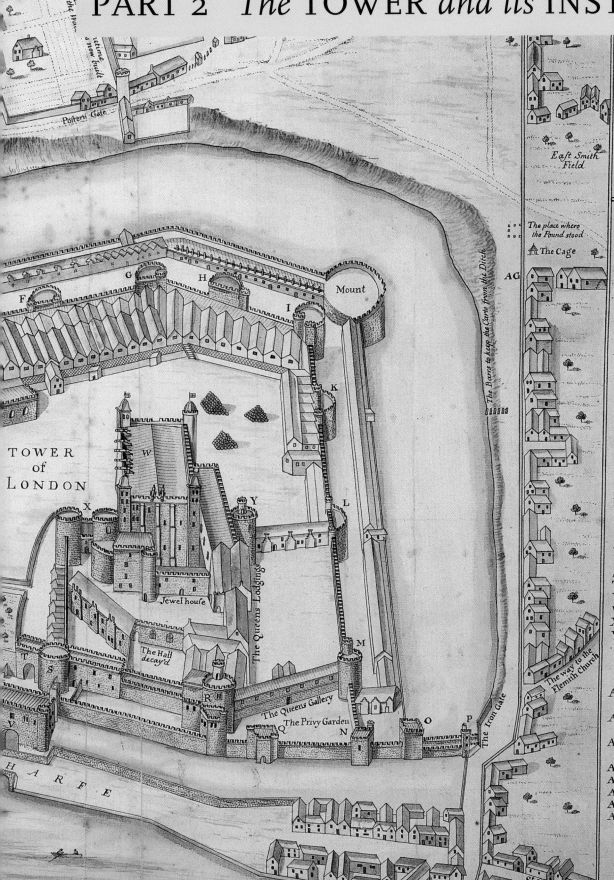

A TRUE and EXACT COP
of the DRAUGHT of the
TOWER LIBERTIE
Surveyd in the year 159
by GULIELMUS HAIWAR
and J. GASCOYNE.

The Liberties of the Tower beginning at
Water Gate next the Rams Head in Petty Wa
doth extend straight North to the end of Torve
Street and direct North to the Mud Wall calle
Pikes Garden on this side the Crutched Fryers a
so straight East to the Wall of London with the Ni
Gardens above the Postern and above the Broken To
right unto the midst of Hog Lane and and so stra
broad South to the Stone Corner and so on to ÿ Tham
and according to the former abutting a green line
drawn about the said liberties.

Where there is not sufficient room for names of pla
ces to be written, the names of such places are no
ted with letters and are to be referr'd to ÿ Alphab
ical table here under written.

These are the Marks of the
Several Towers.

A. The Middle Tower.
B. The Tower at the Gate.
C. The Bell Tower.
D. Buecamp Tower.
E. Devilin Tower.
F. Flint Tower.
G. Bowyar Tower.
H. Brick Tower.
I. Martin Tower.
K. Constable Tower.
L. Broad Arrow Tower.
M. Salt Tower.
N. Well Tower.
O. The Tower leading to the Iron Gate.
P. The Tower above Iron Gate.
Q. The Cradle Tower.
R. The Ianthorn Tower.
S. The Hall Tower.
T. The Bloody Tower.
V. St Thomas Tower.
W. Cæsar's, or White Tower.
X. Cole Harberte
Y. Warderoap Tower.

These are the Marks for the
Boundaries of the Liberties

A B. The House at the Water Gate call'd the
Rams Head.
A C. The place where the Mud Wall was call'd
Pikes Garden.
A D. The City Wall at the North East of the
Nine Gardens
A E. The place where the Broken Tower was
A F. Hog Lane end.
A G. The House call'd the Stone corner House.
A H. The End of Tower Street.
A I. The Stairs without the East end of the
Tower.

The ROYAL LODGINGS 1485–1604

Last repaired by Henry VIII, parts of the lodgings are saved from conversion or abandonment until the seventeenth century by their symbolic significance and their place in royal ritual.

LEFT 56. The earliest non-schematic image of the Tower of London, from a late fifteenth-century book of poems by Charles, Duke of Orléans. Captured at Agincourt in 1415 and imprisoned at the Tower, he is shown here in the White Tower at the window, seeing the messenger arrive with his ransom and greeting him (centre), signing a formal release (right) and leaving with an escort (left). The view is particularly important for its depiction of St Thomas's Tower and the adjoining buildings of the royal lodgings, including the Great Hall and the White Tower, then still white and complete with the twelfth-century 'forebuilding'. London Bridge and the city are shown in the background.

RIGHT 57. Portrait of Henry VIII by Hans Holbein, c. 1536. Henry and his father were the last sovereigns to make improvements to the royal lodgings at the Tower.

Henry VII (1485–1509) and Henry VIII (1509–1547)

Even in the Middle Ages the Tower of London was in fact relatively little used as a residence by the sovereign, for whom Westminster was the more attractive London base. Under the Tudors its importance as a working residence diminished even further, as it became, in the words of the sixteenth-century London chronicler Raphael Holinshed, more "an armourie and house of munition, and thereunto a place for the safekeeping of offenders than a palace roiall for a king or queen to sojourne in". By the end of the Tudor period the palace buildings, neglected since the death of Henry VIII, were virtually uninhabitable. Nevertheless, its occasional use by royalty was to be ensured by the deeply ingrained significance attached to the Tower as a symbol of the continuity and authority of the monarchy.

The first two Tudor monarchs were the last to make any serious attempt to improve or maintain the palace buildings. Henry VII's work was largely intended to provide additional private lodgings of the sort by then thought necessary, placed in a new tower, begun in 1501 – while a gallery and a new garden were added in 1506. At least two of these features can be picked out on the Elizabethan plan of almost a century later (fig. 55): the new tower may be identified with the slender construction shown attached to the outer wall to the west of the Cradle Tower, while the gallery can be seen extending along the top of the south curtain

wall between the Lanthorn and Salt towers (marked as 'The Queens Gallery'). The garden was probably that labelled the 'Privy Garden', to the south of the gallery, or possibly occupied the space to the north. These works created a second court to the east of the old palace complex, with the new gallery intersecting the gardens in the fashionable Continental style.

LEFT In 1536 Anne Boleyn was tried for treason in the Great Hall of the Tower, which had been repaired for her coronation four years before.

RIGHT In James I's reign the King's great chamber was partitioned to create a room 50 ft by 18 ft for the use of the Earl of Northumberland, held prisoner there.

In 1562 military stores were being kept in Elizabeth I's own apartments within the Tower, which were so overloaded, that it was feared the floors would collapse.

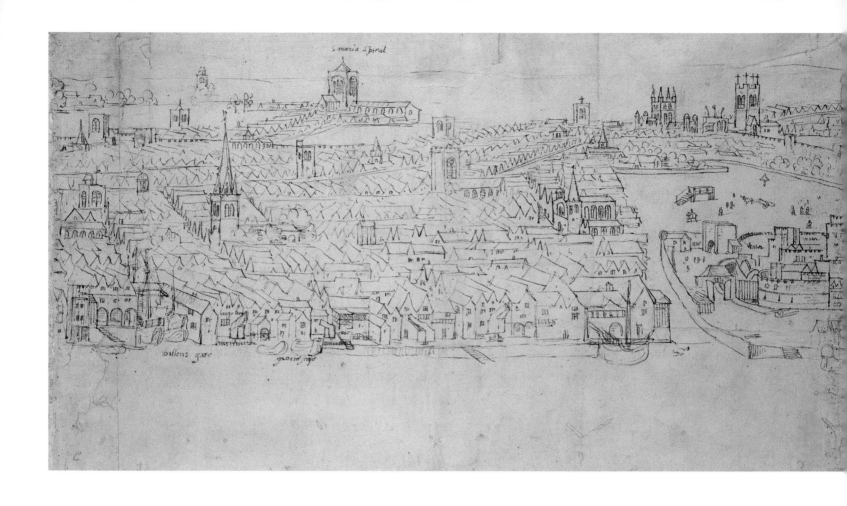

s maria spital

58. *View of the Tower from a panorama by Anthonis van den Wyngaerde of 1544. The royal lodgings can be seen clustered in front and to the right of the White Tower, most of the larger windows denoting rooms added or refurbished under Henry VII and Henry VIII. In the distance to the left is the open space of Tower Hill, with the scaffold standing in the middle.*

Henry VIII's work to the palace represented an attempt not so much to expand the Tower's accommodation, as his father had done in a modest way, but simply to make the main ceremonial rooms serviceable. The greatest effort was made in advance of the coronation of his second wife, Anne Boleyn, in June 1533, which led to a refurbishment of the Great Watching Chamber and Privy Chamber – his guardroom and bedroom. Within the Queen's own apartments, to the north, the principal works were to the Great Chamber, which was given a new roof and floor. References to "Antyk" work suggest that classical motifs were incorporated in the decoration. The celebrations connected with the coronation – among which were to be the ceremonial creation of 18 Knights of the Bath – entailed further works, including the repair and redecoration of Henry III's Great Hall and the overhaul of the kitchens. The lodgings over St Thomas's Tower were also largely rebuilt to accommodate the Lord Great Chamberlain and the Lord Chamberlain, the King's chief household officers. The last, executed according to a contract with the celebrated master carpenter Thomas Nedeham for £120, is all that survives from this period: although restored in the nineteenth century (see p. 118), the timber framing of the north wall and the massive roof structure, designed to carry the weight of cannon, is his work.

The end of royal residence

Following Anne Boleyn's coronation, Henry rarely, if ever, stayed at the Tower again, and Anne only as a prisoner from 2 May 1536 until her execution on the 17th. Thereafter, the monarch stayed there only when the symbolic importance of the castle made this politically useful. Thus, once the death of Henry VIII had been made public, the young Edward VI (1547–1553) was lodged at the Tower for three weeks, and it was from there, in fulfilment of the tradition established in the early fourteenth century (see p. 42), that he processed from the castle to Westminster on the morning of his coronation. The same custom was observed by Queen Mary (1553–1558) for the same reasons, and by Queen Elizabeth (1558–1603), although neither stayed for more than a few days.

The decision of James I (1603–1625) to visit the Tower on the day of his arrival in London from Edinburgh in May 1603, and to stay there for several nights, must have been similarly based. A contemporary account describes how, after having witnessed the cannons on the roof of the White Tower being fired, he was shown the "Armorie, the Wardrobe, the rich Artillerie and the Church", and the next day the "Ordinance-house and after the Mynt-house, and last of all the Lyons". No doubt James was suitably impressed, but the preparations necessary for his anticipated stay on the eve of his coronation in July –

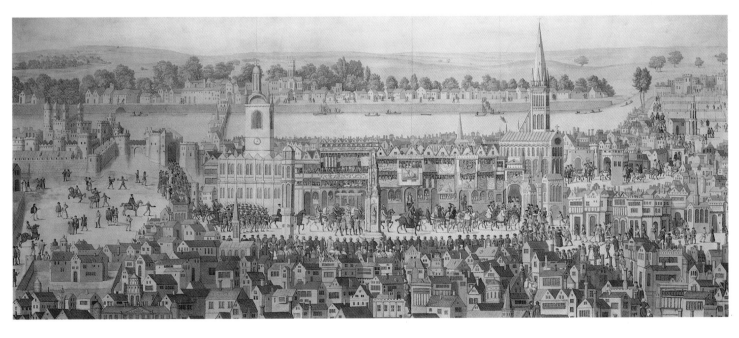

59. *Engraving of a destroyed seventeenth-century view of Edward VI's coronation procession from the Tower to Westminster, which took place on 20 February 1547.*

in the event postponed until 1604 because of an outbreak of plague – show that the lodgings were hardly fit for royal use. The required repairs suggest leaking roofs and a state of general dilapidation, while the Great Hall, in the Middle Ages the architectural showpiece of the palace, was in ruins: derelict since as early as 1559, and shown on the 1597 survey as roofless and "decay'd" (fig. 55), it had to be hastily

given a temporary covering – as is shown by a reference in the building accounts of 1603–04, for the "Frameinge and settinge upp of a sidewall and a roof over the olde hall and raftringe it wth great firpoles to beare a Canvas coveringe being lxx foote in lengthe and xxv foote in bredthe boordinge upp one sidewall". The general shortage of accommodation also required state prisoners, including the disgraced

60. The Arrival of Venetian
Ambassadors at the Tower
Stairs, May 1707, by the
Italian artist Luca Carlevaris.
The practice of greeting
ambassadors and foreign
dignitaries at the Tower derived,

like its use on the eve of the
sovereign's coronation, from
the symbolic significance that
remained attached to the castle
long after it had ceased to be
of practical use as a royal
residence.

adventurer Sir Walter Ralegh, Lord Cobham and
Lord Grey, to be removed to make room for the
King's ministers.

The last sovereign to observe the tradition was
Charles II (1660–1685), who, restored to the throne
in 1660, probably did so in a conscious attempt to
assert the continuity of the monarchy in spite of
the eleven-year Interregnum. However, the arrange-

ments he made underline both the importance attached to the Tower and the irredeemable condition of its accommodation: although unable, as his forbears had done, to stay there on the eve of his grand coronation procession to Westminster from the Tower, Charles rode to the castle's gates at dawn, thereby ensuring that it continued to form the starting-point of the cavalcade.

The piecemeal transformation and demolition of the royal apartments over the following two centuries can be followed through a series of historic views (figs. 55, 61 and 70): the Wakefield Tower and St Thomas's Tower, both dating from the thirteenth century, are now the only survivals.

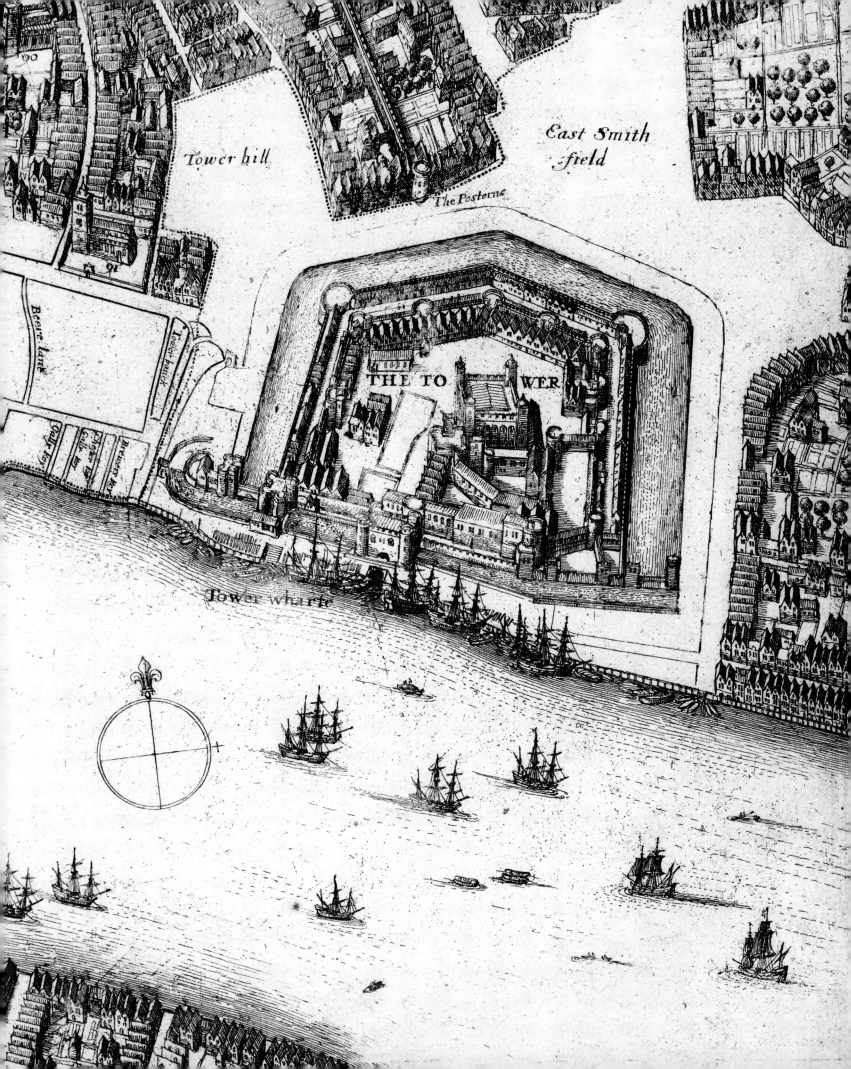

Tower hill

East Smith field

The Posterne

Beere lane

Tower ditch

THE TO WER

Tower wharfe

The ARSENAL
before 1660

Increasingly dominated by the Office of Ordnance and the Office of Armoury, the Tower becomes the nation's greatest store and manufactory of military equipment.

61. Detail from a map engraved by Wenceslaus Hollar after the Great Fire of 1666. Stretching across the full width of the inner bailey to the north of the White Tower is the Ordnance store-house of 1545–47, replaced by the Grand Storehouse in 1688–92. Within the former palace precinct to the south of the White Tower may be seen the roof of the massive ware-house created in the shell of the medieval Great Hall.

From the late Middle Ages until the middle of the nineteenth century the most influential occupants of the Tower were the Office of Ordnance and the Office of Armoury, which between them oversaw the Tower's function as an arsenal, and the role of the castle and what happened there is closely bound up with their activities. Both organizations, as explained in more detail above (p. 30), emerged as specialist offshoots of the Wardrobe – the department of state responsible for supplying, storing and administering the king's goods and weaponry – in the fifteenth century. Their immense importance was largely owing to the absence of a standing army until 1661, and which even thereafter had an intermittent presence until the mid-eighteenth century. This made the existence of a permanent and professional administration to procure and store munitions essential if forces raised to meet particular needs were to be effectively equipped. Until the late seventeenth century the Tower remained not only the headquarters of these organizations, but also the country's main military supply base.

The main stores managed by the two offices were, not surprisingly, armour, edged weapons, handguns and ordnance (heavier weapons and cannon) and – very importantly – gunpowder and its ingredients.

The first known activity by either body had been the takeover of existing buildings on the Tower wharf in 1454, but by the end of the century their main 'house of ordnance' already stood where it and

its successors were to remain until 1841 – across the north side of the Inner Ward, facing the White Tower. The creation of the existing roof to the White Tower and the insertion of a new floor beneath it – recently tree-ring dated to the 1490s – was almost certainly also carried out to provide additional storage space, as there are no fireplaces or other features suggesting domestic use at this level. In 1536, however, the medieval 'house of ordnance', when inspected by the Surveyor of the King's Works (responsible to the king for the building and maintenance of his properties) and the Master of the Ordnance, was found to be in a perilous state and "redy to ffall", and they recommended its replacement. Exactly how "redy" is arguable, for it survived until funds were finally issued to Sir Francis Flemyng, Lieutenant of the Ordnance, to "erect and newe buylde one howse wherein all the Kinges Ordinance and other Municions maye be kepte" in 1545. The result was, at least in plan, the Tower's largest ever building, as is clearly shown by the 1597 survey, Hollar's view of 1666, and the plan of 1682 and its derivatives (figs. 55, 61 and 92). Sir Francis's accounts tell us that it was built of timber on a brick footing, equipped with brick chimneys, tiled roofs, lead gutters, and provided with racks for hanging weapons – some in special rooms "wherein all the Kinges maieties riche Weapons of his own person should be kepte".

The 1560s saw the first of a renewed series of incursions into areas and buildings formerly belong-

In 1588 the Earl of Leicester complained that the helmets he received from the Tower stores were in so poor a state that his men were ashamed to wear them.

LEFT A Swiss visitor to the Tower in 1599 was shown "the actual armour of King Henry, the which was mighty burdensome"; this can still be seen at the Tower today.

RIGHT In Elizabeth I's reign the monopoly for supplying gunpowder to the crown was held by George Evelyn, grandfather of the diarist John Evelyn.

62. *Medal struck by the Flemish medallist Jan Roettier for Charles II (1660–1685) as one of a planned series commemorating the sufferings of royalists during the Interregnum. The face shown depicts the north elevation of the White Tower and the various doorways and hatches cut through it in the preceding decades to facilitate the movement of stores in and out of the building.*

presumably the medieval undercroft or cellar (fig. 61). Storage facilities in the White Tower were also improved when, in 1565–66, the Armoury Office fitted out two armouries with hundreds of wooden 'crosses' on which armours were mounted.

A special "Powderhous" is mentioned in the Tower as early as 1461, but towards the end of Elizabeth I's reign much, if not all, the gunpowder in the fortress was being stored in the White Tower, and in 1594 hatches were fitted in the powder-room floor, through which barrels could presumably be hoisted from ground level. Further adaptations followed in 1603–04 with the replacement of the fifteenth-century floor to the topmost western room by the existing structure, and the insertion of posts to support the floors and the roof. In 1610 facilities for storing powder outside the White Tower were increased, with the construction of a dedicated building somewhere in the Mint in the Outer Ward. In 1636 another part of the White Tower was converted into a powder store and a large doorway punched through the external wall to allow supplies to be hoisted directly into the building from the outside – probably the large doorway with splayed reveals in the north wall of the eastern chamber on the first floor (fig. 63). The next two years saw the first of a series of major alterations to the White Tower's external appearance, with the replacement of much of its cut-stone work and window surrounds with Portland stone (a hard, white material from Dorset), while in 1639 the whole of the exterior of the building was whitewashed – perhaps for the last time. In 1657 yet another part of the White Tower, possibly

ing to the royal lodgings, made possible by their virtual abandonment after the death of Henry VIII (see p. 52), beginning with the fitting up of stores in "the Queenes chamber within her graces lodging". In the seventeenth century the takeover of the old palace buildings speeded up still further, in 1639 its largest building, the 'old hall', being converted into a storehouse for guns, carriages and other equipment: three floors were inserted into the empty shell, carried on timber uprights, with elaborate measures being taken to overcome the difficulties caused by the "many vaults being formerly buried there"–

63. *Opening in the north wall of the White Tower at first-floor level, widened in 1636 to create a doorway through which gunpowder could be hoisted in from outside.*

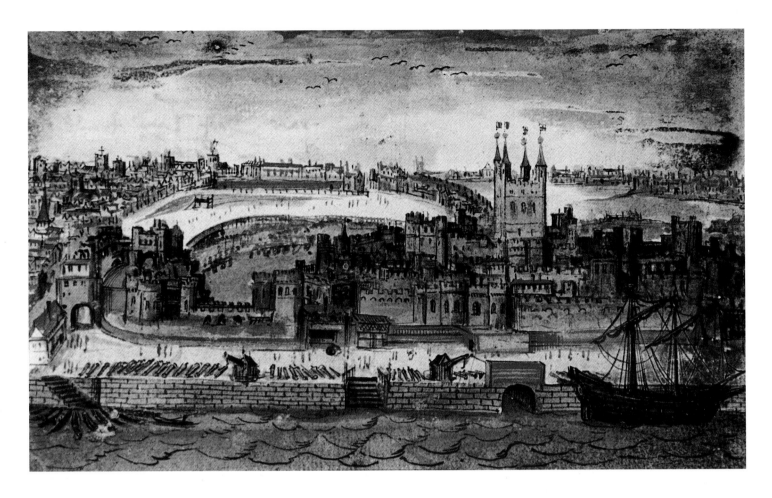

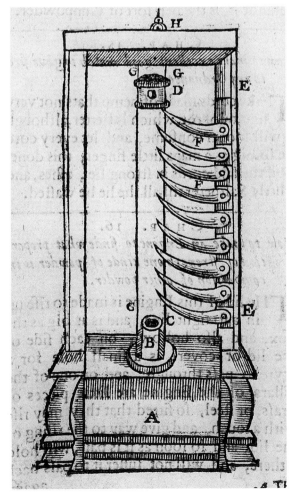

ABOVE 64. *A view of 1615 by Michael van Meer, giving a good impression of the castle and its surroundings, although fanciful in some detail, particularly in the depiction of the White Tower. In the foreground, on the wharf, are two cranes for loading munitions and other goods from the arsenal on to ships such as that shown to the right; between them lie the guns of the saluting battery, ready to be fired off on important occasions. In the background is the scaffold and the open space of Tower Hill, with the churches and houses of the city beyond.*

RIGHT 65. *Illustration from Nathaniel Nye's* Art of Gunnery *of 1647, showing a device for measuring or proving the explosive strength of gunpowder. As his text explains, the power of the detonation in the box at the base of the instrument was measured by the distance it was driven up the central pole – calibrated by a series of catches that prevented it from falling back.*

the uppermost eastern chamber, was fitted up by the Ordnance carpenter for the "safe keepeing of a great quantity of powder", thus completing, with the exception of the chapel, the conversion of the whole building into a military storehouse.

In addition to the storage of gunpowder, from at least the early seventeenth century onwards the Tower also provided facilities for testing or 'proving' its explosive strength. In 1610 a 'proof house' was constructed somewhere among the Mint buildings in the Outer Ward, a facility moved in 1650 to the courtyard within the large stone building annexed to the east side of the White Tower. In the same year it was ordered that the Wardrobe premises put up for Henry VIII between the Broad Arrow and Wardrobe towers (fig. 55), conveniently close by, should be fitted up "for the safe keeping of the powder that is to be prooved".

The ARSENAL
after 1660

Although its storage capacity is soon to be outstripped by demand, in the 1660s the Tower establishes its long-lived pre-eminence as a centre of military administration.

66. View of the White Tower from the south-east in the 1870s. The low crenellated building to the left is the Horse Armoury, put up in 1825 to house the Line of Kings (see p. 100), and demolished in 1883. To the right is the eastern annexe, probably of fourteenth-century origin, but shown here as altered in the eighteenth and nineteenth centuries. It was pulled down in 1879. The rounded tower at the corner of the annexe incorporates the remains of the twelfth-century Wardrobe Tower, itself of Roman origin.

In the decades after the restoration of the monarchy in 1660, the Tower of London lost its position as the greatest arsenal in the country: the defence of an expanding overseas empire, and the struggles with France and Spain that followed the replacement of James II (1685–1688) – who, as a Catholic, was a more natural ally – by William III (1689–1702) and Mary II (1689–1694) in 1688, required larger facilities than the Tower could provide. As a result, the Ordnance embarked on the rapid development of sites such as Plymouth, Portsmouth, Chatham and Woolwich, better positioned to supply the massive land- and sea-based operations of the period. But at the same time the authority of the Board of Ordnance, which became responsible for all fortifications in the British Isles in 1667 and took over the Office of Armoury in 1671, was increased still further. At the Tower – still their main administrative base – this required and enabled a rapid expansion of their storage and office accommodation. By 1700 this had caused the overall plan of the fortress, or at least the buildings inside it, to change quite dramatically, as a comparison, for example, between figs. 55 and 83 will quickly show.

Ordnance stores and offices

At the Restoration, with the recall of arms accumulated during the Civil War and the Interregnum, the available storage at the Tower was found to be inadequate. The situation was reviewed by the Privy Council as early as 1661, and it is probably thanks to this that a royal warrant was issued on 17 January 1663 authorising the construction of a new storehouse in that "void peece of ground ... comonly knowne or called by the name of the wardrobe Garden" as "soone as the season will permit": the result, known since the 1950s as the New Armouries building, still stands against the rear of the curtain wall between the Broad Arrow and Salt towers (fig. 68). By the autumn of 1664 craftsmen had been paid for "oyleing ffixinge and cleaneing the Arms" that were transferred into the building from the White Tower; a few weeks later, on 8 November, the naval official and diarist Samuel Pepys noted that, with the addition of the new building, the Tower storehouses were "a noble sight".

The next phase of work concentrated on the immediate surroundings of the White Tower, with the aim of safeguarding it and its vast stocks of gunpowder from fire. As early as 1661 it had been suggested that a safety corridor 6 m (20 ft) wide be created around the White Tower and its eastern annexe to isolate it from danger, but nothing was carried out. The Great Fire of September 1666 (fig. 67), however, which it was feared might reach the White Tower, led to a belated revival of the scheme, and by 1669 the construction of a protective wall and palisade around the building and its eastern annexe was under way. Meanwhile, spurred on by the demands of the Second Dutch War (1665–67), a

Between 1667 and 1704 the number of officers attached to the Ordnance Office grew from 175 to 450.

At the Restoration the Tower was the most important arsenal in the country, and was described to Charles II as "almost your single Magazine".

In the fourteenth century crossbows were mounted on the roofs of the Tower. These were later replaced by guns; a plan of 1682 indicates positions for over 130 guns.

Mortar Peices put upon the Tower

passage was made from the White Tower to the wharf and a new gate and drawbridge created on the south curtain, on the understanding that this would reduce the time to supply a fleet at anchor in the Thames from twenty days to four. In the event, however, the scheme was swiftly abandoned and the gate blocked up, no doubt in the fear of a repeat of the daring and successful Dutch raid up the River Medway in 1667.

Further demolition of buildings against the White Tower followed in the 1670s, including, in 1674, "pullinge down the Tower against the White Tower" – almost certainly the twelfth-century forebuilding: in the process, the remains of two skeletons were found and identified as those of the murdered Edward V and his younger brother (see pp. 46–47). The demolition of the thirteenth-century Coldharbour Gate followed in 1675, with the lead being sent off for re-use at the new Royal Observatory, then being built at Greenwich. The remains of the Tudor Jewel House, along with other remnants of the royal lodgings and various buildings occupied by Yeoman Warders and others were also swept away: in the following year the exterior of the White Tower and its eastern annexe – now free of accretions – was repaired, and a new staircase built into the south front giving direct access to the record office in the Chapel of St John the Evangelist.

While the demolition of old buildings was under way, new ones were going up, including, by July 1670, a two-storey brick-built storehouse in the Palace Ward: probably identifiable as the 'Little Storehouse' shown on the 1688 survey against its western curtain wall (fig. 70), this was finished by April 1672, when the Ordnance carpenter was "fitting up the Traine of Artilery" inside. The continuing demand for storage space resulted in a small storehouse being erected at the west end of the wharf in 1669–70 and, in 1685–86, long rows of timber sheds put up against the palisades to the east, west and south of the White Tower, and across the east side of the Palace Ward, facing the New Armouries building. These relatively minor structures, however, were soon to be completely overshadowed by the gigantic Grand Storehouse, which towered over the north side of the castle until its tragic destruction in 1841 (see p. 101). The need for such a building became apparent in January 1687, when the Master-General of the Ordnance, George Legge, was advised of the "crazy condition"

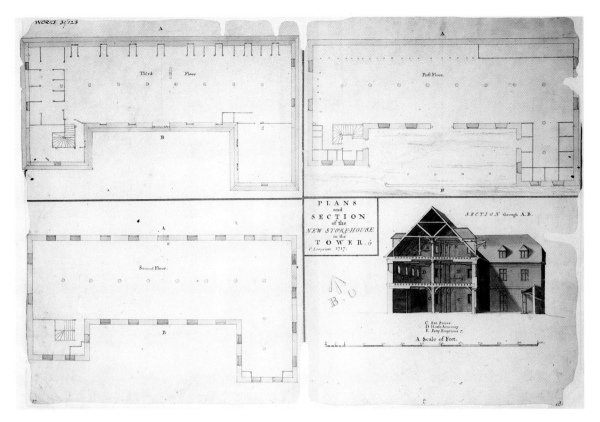

69. *Plan and section through the New Armouries building in 1717. The large bare interiors clearly reveal its function as a warehouse, as does the capstan on the top floor, used to winch heavy loads up to doorways on the west front. The B.O stamped on to the drawing stands for Board of Ordnance, as does the 'Broad Arrow' symbol above it – used by the Ordnance since the sixteenth century and today still used as a mark of government ownership.*

70. Draught of the Tower raised in perspective *by the Ordnance engineer Holcroft Blood in 1688, as engraved in 1815. The recently completed New Armouries building by then occupied the south-east corner of the Inner Ward (lower right), but the Tudor Long House of Ordnance, soon to be demolished, still stood to the north of the White Tower.*

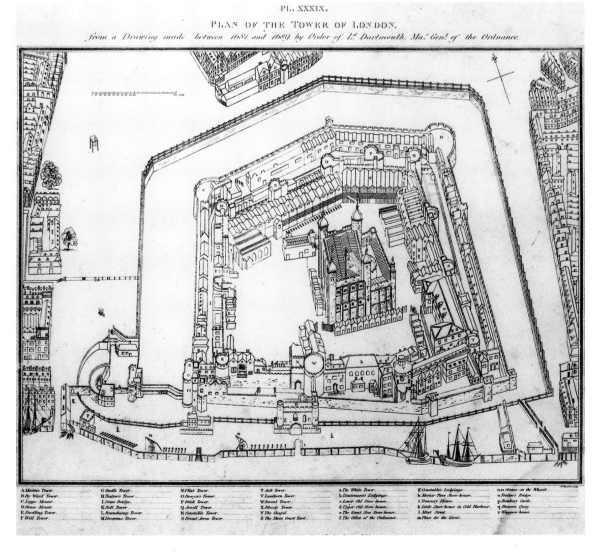

PL. XXXIX.

PLAN OF THE TOWER OF LONDON,

from a Drawing made between 1681 and 1689, by Order of Ld. Dartmouth. Maj. Genl. of the Ordnance.

of the sprawling sixteenth-century storehouses to the north of the White Tower: after a year's deliberation it was decided to replace them with a single new structure, and on 1 March 1688 Legge ordered the work to begin. Completed four years later, the new building was of brick with Portland stone dressings, nearly 110 m (360 ft) long, 18 m (60 ft) wide, three storeys high, and of considerable architectural pretension – the *pièce de résistance* being the frontispiece and pediment to the south front (figs. 72 and 75). Its design, often attributed to Sir Christopher Wren, or to the principal building contractor, Thomas Fitch, was almost certainly the work of an engineer among the Ordnance staff.

In addition to storage, the Ordnance also had a growing demand for office space, and in 1672–73 the builders were busy preparing new premises in the Palace Ward to replace their old offices behind the Chapel of St Peter ad Vincula. The T-shaped building stood immediately north of the Lanthorn Tower and to the east of the former medieval Great Hall (converted into an Ordnance store in 1641), and incorporated part of the medieval Queen's Lodgings: it was evidently ready for occupation by the end of September 1673, when the officers and clerks were instructed to "remove all their Bookes, papers and writeings to the new Office ... without ffayle".

In contrast to the prolific building activity of the late seventeenth century, the early years of the next were relatively quiet. The re-appointment of the Duke of Marlborough as Master-General of the Ordnance in October 1714 and the Scottish rebellion led by James II's son, the 'Old Pretender', that broke out the following year, however, signalled the start of renewed works at the Tower – part of a bustle of military activity throughout the country. Between 1715

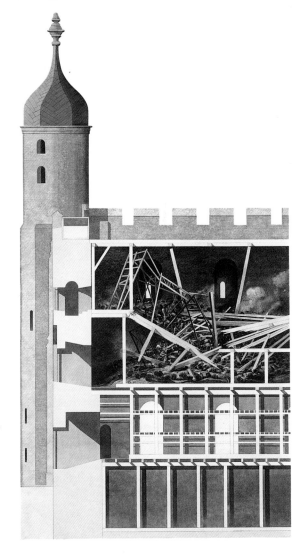

71. *The dangers of storing large quantities of gunpowder were vividly demonstrated on the morning of 9 July 1691, when the floor of the powder room in the White Tower collapsed, sending some 2000 barrels crashing down on to the floor below, as shown in this modern reconstruction.*

72. *The pediment sculpture from the Grand Storehouse carved by John Young in 1691 and seen here mounted on a wall near the Martin Tower in the 1920s. The arms of William III (1689–1702), supported by a lion and a unicorn, are flanked by assorted items of military equipment, reflecting the building's function as an arsenal.*

and 1717 considerable efforts were made to improve the storage facilities in and about the White Tower. In February 1715 the Board ordered the western basement to be fitted out to receive saltpetre (the main ingredient of gunpowder) purchased from the East India Company, and two months later the floor of the eastern compartment was lowered to provide additional space. In addition, the medieval openings to the ground floor were considerably enlarged and, together with those on the upper floor, fitted with the existing Portland stone architraves, frequently but wrongly attributed to Wren: the windows on the first floor were formed to the same pattern later in the eighteenth century. At the same time, four new doorways, with matching stone surrounds, were formed in the north front to allow easier movement of stores in and out of the building. Between 1729 and 1733 the White Tower facilities were again improved, this time with the insertion of the existing brick vaults across the two principal basement rooms, to provide greater security for saltpetre storage. The existing timber floors in the upper parts of the building also date from this campaign, while the eastern annexe was once again refurbished and its accommodation extended into its internal courtyard.

In the nineteenth century there were some major operations in support of the Tower's role as a military supply depot, but also, after the 1850s, there was a steady decline in its importance. Among the most important initiatives was the construction in 1834 of a tramway to convey military stores from the wharf directly into the White Tower, which involved the opening of a new gateway in the south curtain to the east of St Thomas's Tower and the building of a draw-bridge across the south moat, on the site of the short-lived crossing of 1667; from this point the supply route passed through the late eighteenth-century storehouse, to the east of the Wakefield Tower, and along a tunnel, before entering the basement of the White Tower near the south-west corner. Further works took place during the Crimean War of 1853–56, although the Board of Ordnance, a scapegoat for its slow progress, was dissolved by Act of Parliament in 1855 and its duties transferred to the War Office; the Board's splendid offices in the Palace Ward were given several extra floors and converted into a giant store-house, while temporary warehouses were erected in

ABOVE 73. The arms of the Board of Ordnance, mounted on the south wall of the New Armouries building. Made of an artificial material (Coad stone), they were originally placed over the main entrance of the Ordnance Office in 1779 (see fig. 74).

RIGHT 74. Artist's impression of the north front of the Ordnance Office in about 1800, with the storehouse of 1663–64 (the New Armouries building) beyond. The office erected in 1777–80 can be seen with Eleanor Coad's trophy of arms set in the pediment over the portico; to the right is the extension of 1789–92.

BELOW 75. Drawing by the Ordnance Engineer John Hanway of about 1710, showing the south elevation of the Grand Storehouse, completed in 1692.

The largest single building operation undertaken by the Ordnance at the Tower in the eighteenth century, however, was the reconstruction of their office in the Palace Ward, following a fire in January 1774. The site clearance, which, two years later, pre-ceded construction, saw the removal of much of what remained of the old medieval and Tudor palace, including the thirteenth-century Lanthorn Tower, damaged beyond repair. The new office was a hand-some Neoclassical building measuring 32 x 30.5 m (105 x 100 ft), arranged around a small courtyard, with the main entrance to the north, surmounted by a pediment and the arms of the Board of Ordnance (fig. 73). Ready for occupation in the autumn of 1780, it was soon seriously damaged by another fire in July 1788, and was being repaired and substantially mod-ified by January 1789: four years later, in addition to a complete recasting of the interior, it had been extended by 13 m (45 ft) to the west at the expense of the storehouse, which had been improvised within the shell of the medieval Great Hall. In addition, a new storehouse was erected to the west of the enlarged office (fig. 78).

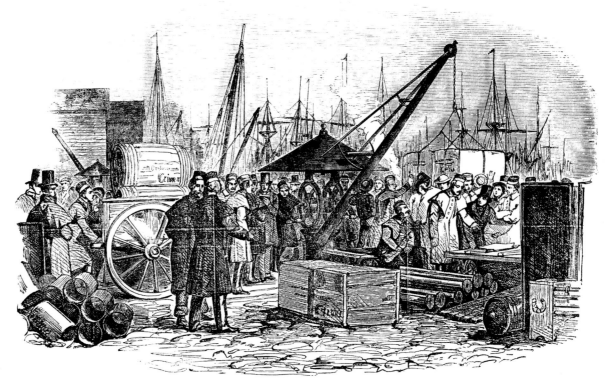

the eastern moat and on ground immediately to the west of the Salt Tower. After the end of the war, however, the buildings became progressively redundant and none of them survived the restoration of the castle in the second half of the century.

Ordnance lodgings

The Ordnance not only required storage space within the castle, but also lodgings for the various officials who were required, as set out in their Instructions of 1683, to "make their Ordinary Habitation and Aboad in the houses and Lodgeings Assigned them in or neare the Tower". The most senior, the Master of the Ordnance, had his residence installed in the thirteenth-century Brick Tower along the northern inner curtain wall around 1510–20 (the use of brick on this occasion giving it its name); this remained the official residence until just before the outbreak of the Civil War in 1641, when he was provided with more commodious and prestigious accommodation in former royal lodgings in and about the Lanthorn Tower. Other officials were provided with accommodation as befitted their rank, including, at the lowest end of the scale, the Ordnance Labourer. These lodgings were scattered all over the Tower, but many were located against the rear of the curtain wall between

The Tower from the Thames in about 1660, on the eve of the major expansion and improvement of its supply and storage facilities carried out under Charles II (1660–1685) and his brother James II (1685–1688). The small warship in the foreground is a reminder that the Tower was an important supply centre for sea as well as land forces. Tinted drawing by Wenceslaus Hollar.

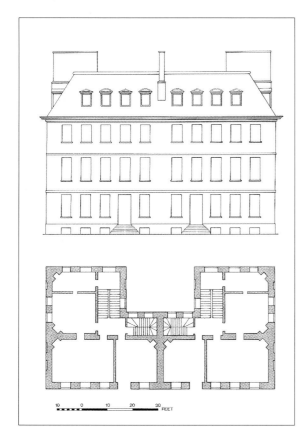

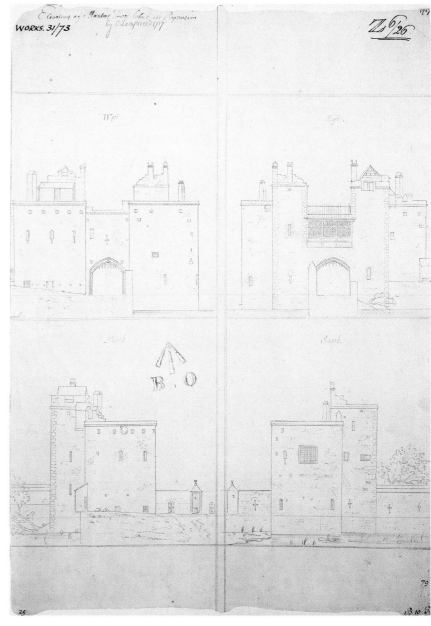

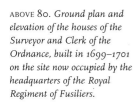

ABOVE 80. *Ground plan and elevation of the houses of the Surveyor and Clerk of the Ordnance, built in 1699–1701 on the site now occupied by the headquarters of the Royal Regiment of Fusiliers.*

RIGHT 81. *Elevations of the Middle Tower prepared by the Ordnance surveyor Clement Lemprière in 1717, immediately prior to its refurbishment in 1717–19 for the Ordnance Barrack Master. The east elevation (top right) is of interest in showing, in section, the medieval south parapet to the causeway and the large, late medieval window overlooking it.*

82. *The lock (firing mechanism) of a flint-lock Short Land Pattern musket of about 1785, assembled at the Tower, and marked* Tower *beside the cypher of King George III.*

83. *View of the Tower from the east in 1804 by T. Daniell and W. Daniell. In the foreground are the buildings of the 'Arms manufactory', put up to cope with the extra demand for small arms following the outbreak of the Napoleonic Wars in 1803.*

the Martin and Broad Arrow towers, adjoining or near the Lanthorn Tower and in and about the Devereux Tower. Much of the work associated with these lodgings during the late Stuart period was confined to repair and refurbishment, but a few new buildings were erected; by far the most prodigious of these was a pair of great houses for the Surveyor and the Clerk of the Ordnance, built between 1699 and 1701 on the site now occupied by the headquarters of the Royal Regiment of Fusiliers (fig. 80).

There was rather more activity in the eighteenth century: in 1715 the dilapidated state of the Middle Tower (fig. 81), by now the official residence of the Ordnance Barrack Master, gave rise to concern, and some of its defective battlements were taken down in an attempt to ease the problem. More radical measures followed, and between 1717 and 1719 the medieval timber framing to the rear of the gate-tower was removed, the exterior walls partially refaced with Portland stone, round-headed windows inserted, and the existing arms of George I placed over the outer gateway. In the years either side of 1720 several new lodgings were built for Ordnance officials, the most imposing being the so-called Old Hospital Block to the north of the New Armouries building, built in 1718–19 to house four clerks. The only other surviving eighteenth-century Ordnance lodging is the house built in 1735 for a clerk named Mr Offley overlooking Tower Green, now the official residence of the Tower doctor.

Ordnance workshops

In addition to its role as a storehouse, the Tower was also used for the assembling, finishing and testing of small arms or hand-held guns, although generally using parts supplied by contractors and made elsewhere. In the eighteenth century the Tower craftsmen also supplied patterns on which outside contractors could model their products, and provided training in using them.

Activity of this sort, managed since the sixteenth century by the Small Gun Office, had long been a feature of Tower life, but the sale of the old Artillery Ground in the Minories, north of the Tower, in 1682 saw the transfer of operations associated with the proving (testing) of small guns to the Tower, and a new "Proofe house and Chargeing house upon Tower wharfe" was begun in August 1682. Further workshop space was provided in the early eighteenth century near the Devereux Tower, while additional facilities were installed in the Flint and Bowyer towers in 1718, one tower being fitted out for "stocking", the other for "Lock hardening". In addition, forges were provided for their use in the Mint and on the wharf, and a water-powered machine for drilling out gun barrels was installed in St Thomas's Tower in the 1720s.

The outbreak of the Napoleonic Wars in 1803 and the enormous increase in the demand for guns was more than the existing Ordnance supply system could cope with, so an 'Arms Manufactory', employ-

84. *Drawing of the interior of the Lock Room on the upper floor of the Flint Tower in November 1841. Gunsmiths had been repairing and maintaining musket locks in the building since the Ordnance set up a workshop here in 1718.*

ing hundreds of people, was established at the eastern end of the wharf around the old Proof House (fig. 83). The factory closed in 1815 when the office's manufacturing facilities were transferred to Enfield and Lewisham. The buildings, however, were left standing to house the department's workshops – much to the annoyance of the military engineers, who, throughout the first half of the nineteenth century, repeatedly called for their demolition to improve the defences of the Tower.

The Drawing Room and the Ordnance Survey

An important but little-known development at the Tower at the start of the reign of George I (1714–1727) was the creation of the Ordnance Drawing Room, which made a major contribution to the training of British military surveyors and draughtsmen in the eighteenth century and was the precursor of the existing Ordnance Survey.

During the seventeenth century surveying and draughting for the Office of Ordnance was the pre-

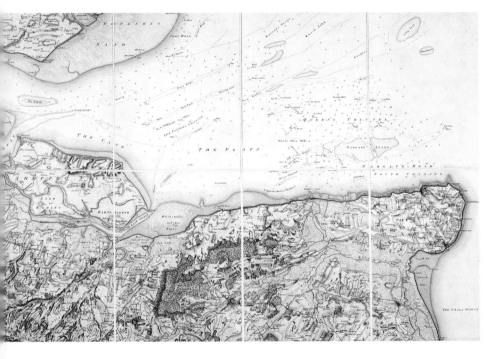

serve of the engineers, whose duties were to provide designs for new military establishments and fortifications, and drawings of existing ones at home and abroad. In 1712, however, the Ordnance effectively created an independent subsection with the appointment of a certain Robert Whitehand as a "Draughtsman ... Constantly to attend the Office". Early staff included, from July 1716, Andrews Jelfe, who was joined the following December by the highly talented Clement Lemprière, whose association with the Tower was to span nearly forty years. Their arrival was preceded by the decision in February 1716 to establish the Drawing Room on the first floor of the large stone building attached to the east side of the White Tower, and it was here that the skills and reputation of the Drawing Room were to develop during the next 150 years. By the time of Lemprière's death in 1746, the Chief Draughtsman had a permanent staff of six, but work relating to the production of a military map of Scotland, ordered after the suppression of the 1745 rebellion, rapidly led to a further increase, and by the early 1780s numbers had risen to fifty. The resulting demand for space was answered by commandeering one of the large houses that had been erected in 1699–1701 opposite the east side of the White Tower (fig. 80).

The Scottish survey, finished in the first instance by 1755, was executed by the distinguished surveyor William Roy, later Lieutenant-Colonel of the Royal Engineers. Roy then formulated a plan for a survey of the whole of the British Isles, and although nothing was done for almost thirty years, in 1784 he was asked to resolve a dispute about the relative positions of the astronomical observatories in Paris and at Greenwich. In doing so he established a series of trigonometrically fixed reference points over the south-east of England, an exercise that encouraged the authorities to back his earlier scheme with a formal government-sponsored programme; in 1791 the Master-General of the Ordnance was given the task of establishing a new controlled survey of the whole country, the aim being to produce accurate maps for the military and the publication of others for general public use. By the mid-1790s a corps of surveyors had been established, "subject to the rules and disciplines of war" and based at the Tower, accompanied from 1801 onwards by a number of engravers, who transferred the drawn surveys to copper sheets for printing. The earliest official product – and the first of the famous Ordnance Survey one-inch (c. 1:50,000) map series – was the map of Kent, engraved for the Master-General by William Faden, an established map-engraver, and published in 1801.

During the next forty years the work of the surveyors, draughtsmen and engravers continued to be managed and carried out from the Tower of London, although there were changes in the status and

TOP 85. *View by Paul Sandby (see fig. 87) of a party of Ordnance surveyors in the Scottish Highlands, working on the survey ordered after the rebellion of 1745. The instrument in the foreground is a theodolite, used for measuring the relative angles between fixed points – the basis of trigonometrical surveying; in the background two men are using chains to record the distance between the instrument and the fixed points (marked by flags).*

ABOVE 86. *Section of a map of Kent surveyed by the Board of Ordnance and engraved for them by William Faden. The scale of one inch to the mile (c. 1:50,000) was used for the published maps that began to be produced in large numbers by the Ordnance Survey after 1841, the year it became independent of the Board.*

87. *View showing the east side of the Middle Tower in 1747, painted by Paul Sandby, a distinguished draughtsman to the Board of Ordnance. Like much work emanating from the Tower Drawing Room, Sandby's was both technically and artistically accomplished.*

88. *Plans and sections made by Clement Lemprière in 1717 of the old building attached to the east side of the White Tower, with the newly fitted-out 'Drawing Room' for the storage, preparation and copying of maps and related material on the upper floor.*

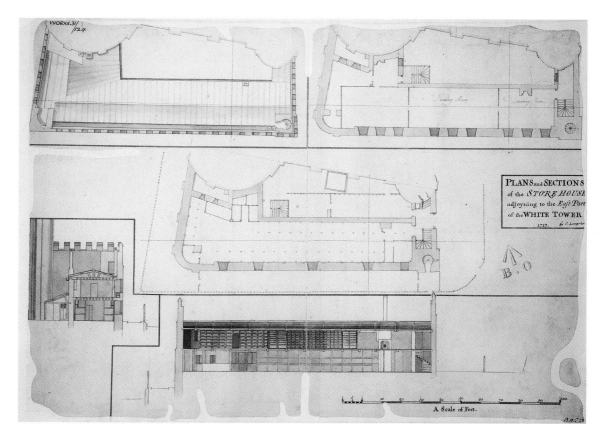

administration of the organization, and for financial reasons the production of one-inch maps was halted between 1811 and 1817, and between 1824 and 1840. In 1841, however, the Ordnance Survey was formally established as a separate organization, and left the Tower for new premises in Southampton.

The GARRISON and FORTIFICATIONS

Recurrent steps are taken to adapt the Tower's medieval ramparts to resist and to carry guns, and to modernize its manning and garrison.

89. View of the Tower from the west of c. 1691 by Johann Spilberg II (detail), showing the medieval walls and towers, now capped with brick embrasures, bristling with newly installed cannon. In the foreground are the remains of the fifteenth-century Bulwark, largely demolished in 1668–70 and soon to disappear completely.

The Tudor period

The last major works to the defences of the Tower before the Tudor period had been the building of the Bulwark and the postern by the Byward Gate (see p. 46), and although a number of improvements had been made in Henry VIII's reign to the royal lodgings and the re-roofing of the White Tower, not much had been done to the castle's defences. Not surprisingly, then, a survey of the Tower initiated by Henry VIII's minister Thomas Cromwell found that virtually every tower and every intervening stretch of wall required attention, and that 2937 tons of Caen stone and a total £3593 4s 1d would be required to put things right. Yet, in spite of their cost, the works – under way by 1532 – fell far short of bringing the defences up to the standards of the time. No attempt was made to equip the castle with the low, angular bastions that were by then needed to carry and resist artillery, or even to reduce the height of the medieval towers; instead, timber platforms were placed on three of the towers along the northern curtain wall, in two positions over the Mint, on St Thomas's Tower and on top of the White Tower. The only known instance of the new arrangements being used in anger, in Mary I's reign, suggests that they were not terribly effective: when the castle was threatened by Protestant rebels under Sir Thomas Wyatt in February 1544, an anonymous eyewitness noted that, as soon as their approach "was perceyved, ther was shot off out of the White Tower a vi or viii shot, but myssed them, sometymes shoting over and sometimes shoting short".

If the physical form of the Tower's fortifications remained archaic, so too did arrangements for guarding it. Until the advent of the Civil War in 1641 the guard was drawn primarily from the body of Yeoman Warders, the Tower gunners and the unreliable attendance of the men of Tower Hamlets who "owe thier service to the Towre ... for the defence of the same". In 1509 the instructions for the Constable and his deputies required four Yeoman Warders and as many gunners, artificers *etc.* as was deemed necessary to guard the entrance to the Tower from the "first opening of the said gate till the last shutting". In 1555 it was decreed that nine men from the ranks of the Yeoman Warders and gunners were to ward during the day and six at night, and instructions were laid for securing the keys at night – the text of which, as an early account of what has become known as the Ceremony of the Keys, deserves quoting:

> And it is ordered that there shall be a place appointed under Locke and key where in the keys of the gates of the saide Tower shall be laide in the sight of the constable, the porter and two of the Yeoman Warders, or three of them at the least, and by two or three of them to be taken out when the[y] shall be occupied. And the key of that locke or coffer where the keys be, to be kepte by the porter or, in his absence, by the chiefe yeoman warder.

A report on the state of the Tower of 1598 complained that many Yeoman Warders were neglecting their duties, being "given to drunckeness, disorders and quarrells".

John Barkstead, under whom the first permanent garrison was stationed at the Tower, was reported to have buried £7000 of gold there. Despite the efforts of Samuel Pepys and others, it has never been recovered.

Sir John Peyton, Lieutenant of the Tower from 1597 to 1603, complained that it was easy to walk right up to the walls of the fortress as the moat was "in maine perts decayed and passable".

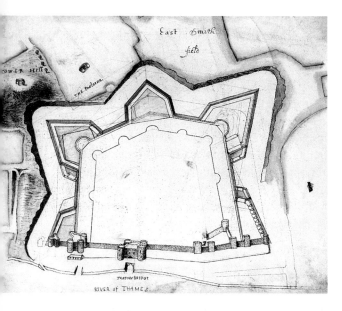

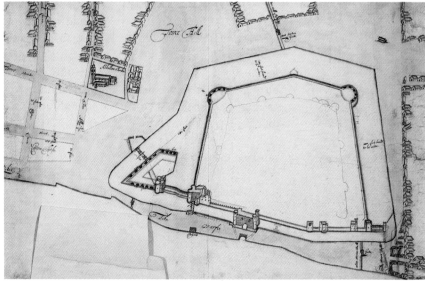

ABOVE LEFT 90. *A scheme for the refortification of the Tower and a realignment of the moat, prepared by the Ordnance Chief Engineer, Sir Bernard de Gomme, in 1666. Had it been carried out, the medieval ramparts on the landward sides would have been augmented by massive bastions, designed to deploy and resist artillery.*

ABOVE RIGHT 91. *A less ambitious scheme for the refortification of the Tower of 1666 by De Gomme. The straightening-up and revetment of the moat's outer edges was carried out in the next two decades, much as shown, but the proposed reinforcement of the western entrance was abandoned.*

The seventeenth century

By the end of the sixteenth century the security of the Tower was being further weakened by private houses and workshops encroaching on the moat and up against the western entrance (fig. 55). The subject of complaints by the Tower authorities as early as 1600, the problem was again considered, in 1620, by six members of the Privy Council, who ordered some immediate action and commissioned another survey, completed at the end of 1623. Once again the principal concern was the moat, the sides of which were found to be encumbered with some 220 houses, sheds, timber yards, coal yards, wheelers' yards and such like. A major dredging operation was also recommended, to be followed by the construction of a brick retaining wall, 4.8 m (16 ft) high and 1.5–2 m (5–6 ft) thick, to restrict further silting. In the event, little if anything was actually done.

In 1640, however, the threat to the Crown posed by the political struggle between Charles I (1625–1649) and parliament led to an attempt to secure the Tower and its vital stores of money and equipment for the King. Charles was in no doubt as to its importance, describing it in the following year as a "bridle upon the city", which was by now openly sympathetic to his opponents. On 15 May 1640 Trained Bands (local militia) were ordered into the castle on the King's behalf, and lodged in canvas-covered huts; in October plans were being prepared for the disposition of ordnance, including twenty-one cannon and three mortars on the White Tower, together with instructions for the gunners. By December a number of gun platforms had been built, and in April the following year carpenters' bills were settled for making "engines" to haul guns on to them, making gun carriages, mounting guns, and for erecting a musket-proof house on "Tower Wall for the Gunners defence". Finally, in May 1641, an account was settled

with the eminent gun founder John Browne for eight pieces of brass ordnance ordered for the roof of the White Tower.

In the event, however, the Tower fell to the Parliamentarians without a shot being fired. Following Charles's ill-advised attempt to arrest five members of the House of Commons in January 1642, and his hasty departure from the capital, Parliament decided to oust the Tower's royalist Lieutenant, Sir John Byron. Blockaded by the citizens of London and the Trained Bands – now also on the side of Parliament – and viewing his position as untenable, Byron sought and received the King's permission to withdraw, and was replaced by Sir John Conyers. Thus, when war actually broke out in November 1642, the castle was already in the hands of rebel sympathisers and its loss, along with that of London, had helped to seal the outcome of the Civil War even before it began.

Following the restoration of the monarchy in 1660, the defences were again inspected, this time by George Monck, now 1st Duke of Albemarle, who once again recommended the dredging of the moat. Whether this was carried out is unclear, but his second recommendation, the removal of the buildings still in place along its edges, was effected with dramatic speed on the night of 4 September 1666: with the Great Fire sweeping through London, the authorities, fearing that the flames would reach the White Tower and its vast store of explosives, had the offending buildings destroyed within hours. The fire was, however, to have a more permanent impact on the Tower. In the general climate of reflection that followed the disaster, the whole question of its defences was considered again, and between 20 and 24 November 1666 Sir Bernard de Gomme, the Ordnance Chief Engineer, was engaged in "makeinge a draught of [the] Tower and designe of fortifieinge the same". His first and most ambitious offering –

reflecting his experience in the Civil War and of Continental warfare in the 1630s – would have completely transformed the castle, bringing its defences up to a contemporary European standard. Although, in the event, the scheme never left the drawing board, some of his other recommendations were carried out. The demolition of the old Bulwark, built to reinforce the western entrance by Edward IV (1461–1483), was begun in November 1668 and replaced in 1670 by a new wall and gate to the north of the Lion Tower. More importantly, improvements to the moat – of the kind recommended in 1623 – were finally carried out, taking the form of a massive brick revetment wall on the western and northern banks, built between July 1670 and December 1672. In 1683 the retaining wall was continued down the east side of the moat, and the entire length of it fenced off with a wooden "Raile ... to prevent peoples

falling in" (fig. 70). The existing revetment masonry to the moat's northern and western arms, though much repaired, is largely of that date.

The garrison's accommodation also received attention at this time, with the construction of the first purpose-built soldiers' lodgings against the curtain wall between the Salt and Broad Arrow towers, on a site otherwise formerly occupied by buildings used to mint coins for Ireland, between 1669 and 1670. Consisting of two storeys and an attic, the 'Irish Barracks', as it was known, was essentially a timber-framed building with a weather-boarded exterior. Further initiatives were taken in the late 1670s and 1680s, resulting from another Privy Council enquiry: in February 1680 contracts were signed with the bricklayers to enlarge the ramparts along the outer south curtain wall and to demolish the old medieval causeway leading from the Iron

92. Detail of a plan of the Tower made in 1681–82, to accompany a report recommending improvements to its defences. The proposed positioning for cannon – largely as executed – are marked by dots.

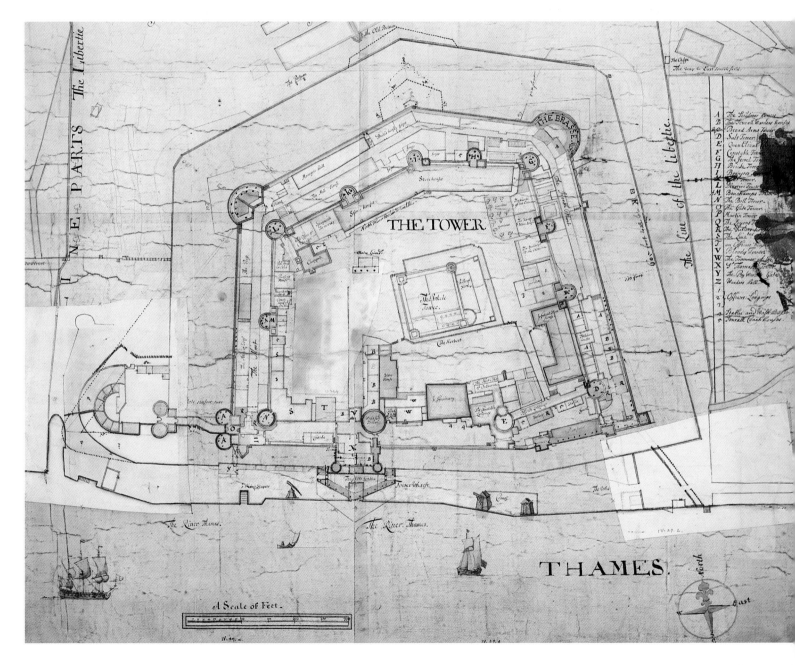

75

RIGHT 93. *View of the Tower in about 1840 by George Bryant Campion, showing the wet moat in its last years. In 1843 it was at last decided that the value of the wet moat as a defensive feature was out-weighed by the health risk that its stagnant waters posed for the garrison, and by 1845 it had been drained and filled in.*

BELOW 94. *Plan and elevation of the Irish Barracks, as redesigned by Dugal Campbell in 1752.*

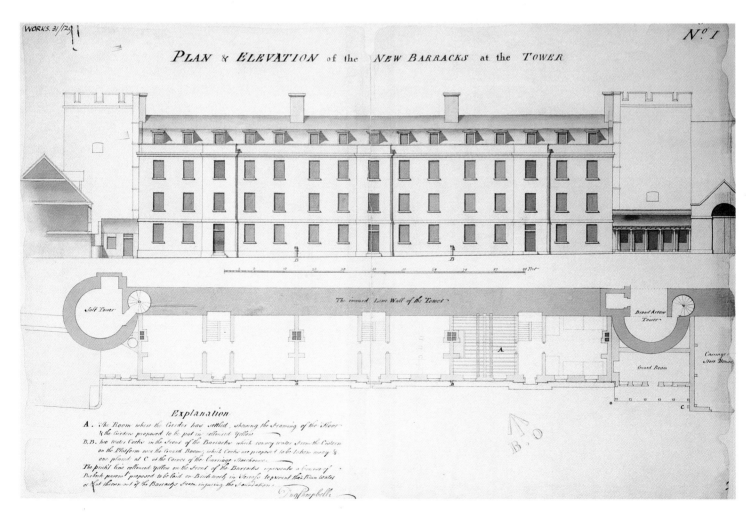

Gate to the Develin Tower so that "the water of the Ditch may Runn round", presumably in the hope that this would reduce the rate of silting. The security of the same area was improved by taking down the Iron Gate and the defensive wall at the east end of the wharf and building a new wall slightly further to the west, as had been recommended by De Gomme in 1666. Finally, the "Old Sally porte" – the Cradle Tower – was ordered to be walled up and about 35 yards of the remaining Bulwark near the wharf taken down after the Board was informed that it was on the point of collapse. Despite these measures, however, the general condition of the Tower's defences and the facilities for the garrison continued to cause concern, and in February 1682 a new series of recommendations for their improvement was laid before the King, which, the minutes tell us, he "was pleased to approve ... & did Order that it be". Over the next six years virtually all thirty-two articles contained in the report were acted upon, representing work on a scale not attempted since the works of 1532–33 (fig. 92).

Against the outer curtain wall, at various locations along the outer landward defences, timber gun platforms were constructed, while on the north-west corner, Legge's Mount was raised some 5 m (19 ft) to its present height to accommodate two tiers of guns (the existing brick gun ports on the first floor date from this time). To the south, a large gun platform was planted on St Thomas's Tower and two smaller devices over the twin towers of the Byward Tower. Similar alterations were made to the mural towers along the three landward sides of the inner curtain wall. Communications between the towers were improved and two sally ports or posterns – both of which survive, although modified – punched through the curtain wall immediately west of the Martin

Tower and midway between the Flint and Devereux towers. Within the walls various coach-houses and stables were converted into accommodation for soldiers and gunners. Another barrack block was built in the Mint opposite the principal lodgings erected in 1669–70. Parts of Legge's Mount were equipped to receive two companies of guards, while a third was quartered in the western half of St Thomas's Tower. Within the Inner Ward a new parade ground was laid out to the north of the Queen's House on the site of the Lieutenant's garden and a bowling-green, while the old Main Guard, located to the south-east of the Beauchamp Tower, was demolished and a new one constructed near the north-west corner of the White Tower. New arrangements were also made for the manning of the Tower's guns, warrants being issued in 1682 to "60 fed Gunners", who were required to lodge within the Tower and exercise as a company under the direction of the Master Gunner of England. This replaced an earlier, and evidently unsatisfactory, arrangement that depended on one hundred part-time gunners.

A permanent garrison in the modern sense had been established during the Interregnum, when as many as eight, but usually six, companies of the regiment, raised by Colonel John Barkstead (the Parliamentary Governor of the Tower), were stationed there. The number during Charles II's reign fluctuated: in 1661 and 1663 there were only three companies, but after 1682 and against a background of political difficulties and the alienation of the City of London the number probably doubled. Improvements were made to their accommodation, but their conduct was also subjected to a set of printed regulations, produced under the Lieutenantship of Sir John Robinson (1660–1679). The long list of instructions included that no officer or soldier should "blas-

95. View of the Tower from the Thames in 1790 by George Dance the younger. The gap in the wharf shown in the foreground was almost certainly associated with the drastic but unsuccessful attempts to improve the maintenance of the moat in the late 1780s.

TOP 96. *The Duke of Wellington laying the foundation-stone of the Waterloo Barracks in 1845.*

ABOVE 97. *Mid-nineteenth-century engraving of the Waterloo Barracks, with the statue of Wellington in the foreground (removed to Woolwich Arsenal in 1863).*

RIGHT 98. *Portrait of the Duke of Wellington by Alfred, Count D'Orsay, 1845. Constable of the Tower from 1826 until 1853, the Duke oversaw many physical changes to the Tower and its administration.*

pheme Gods Holy Name by Oaths, Executions, or Scandalous actions" or "ease themselves in any place than that appointed for that purpose, nor make water within six paces of the Guard, nor throw soile there or ashes, nor empty any pot, nor throw water out of any window". For all offences there were set fines, and for soldiers found drunk on duty the penalty of "riding the horse", and for the improper discharging of muskets within the walls the prospect of enduring three days "in the hole".

Apart from protecting the Tower, troops billeted in the fortress performed the equally important task, in the absence of any true police force, of keeping the peace in surrounding areas. For example, in 1689 and 1696 the Lieutenant of the Tower was ordered to prevent "an unusual concourse of people in Tower hamlets"; a regiment was sent under arms to break up a riot in Southwark in 1693; while four years later troops were dispatched to Westminster to help suppress another riot.

The eighteenth and nineteenth centuries

Further improvements to the defences were initiated in 1714 after the re-appointment of the Duke of Marlborough as Master-General, in response to the precarious position of the newly established Hanoverian dynasty, and the growing threat of a Catholic uprising in Scotland. As work began on the timber gun platforms, which had been installed in 1682–83 and were now seriously decayed, the Surveyor-General produced a report in which the effectiveness of the batteries was reconsidered and the greater part of them judged to be of "no more than appearance". But faced with the considerable cost of replacing seemingly useless defences, it was decided not to renew the platforms, but instead to concentrate all batteries on the outer ramparts. The total number of guns was to be reduced from 118 to 45, a figure, it was observed, that "most Strong Towns in Europe have constantly mounted either in Peace or war" – an observation that was, at best, optimistic: the comment of a Portuguese merchant, presumably familiar with the harsh realities of Continental warfare, that the Tower "would not hold out four and twenty hours against an army prepared for a siege", was probably more realistic.

In April 1752 the accommodation of the Tower garrison came to the fore again after the Irish Barracks, now almost a century old, were deemed beyond repair and had to be replaced. The new building, designed by the Ordnance engineer, Dugal Campbell, was a plain but well-proportioned block measuring some 47.65 x 6.7 m (157 x 22 ft) and comprising three storeys and an attic (fig. 94). Campbell also seems to have designed the Spur Barracks, which provided further soldiers' accommodation on the site of the southern arm of the medieval Lion

99. *The Tower viewed from the roof of a nearby warehouse in 1900, showing the North Bastion of 1856, projecting out into the filled-in moat. In the background is the Royal Mint building of 1810.*

100. *The officers' block, built to complement the soldiers' accommodation in the Waterloo Barracks, and in a similar style, in the late 1840s. It now houses the headquarters of the Royal Regiment of Fusiliers (raised at the Tower in 1685), and the regimental museum.*

Tower moat, by now filled in. At the same time a new guardhouse, known as the Spur Guard, was erected just north of the Middle Tower (fig. 161).

Throughout most of the eighteenth century the built defences of the Tower seem to have been subject to no more than intermittent acts of maintenance and repair. A notable exception was the creation of a new gateway and drawbridge at the east end of the outer southern curtain wall in 1774, giving access from the Outer Ward to the wharf. A certain amount of effort was concentrated on the moat, largely in a vain attempt to combat the perennial problem of silting. Limited attempts were made to scour the moat in 1737 and 1779, but a report of 1787 led to more serious measures being taken two years later, when a channel was cut through the wharf. The aim of this was presumably to allow the tidal waters to carry silt out into the river, but the scheme evidently enjoyed little if any success, and in 1802 the gap was filled in.

In the second quarter of the nineteenth century, however, more drastic action was taken, under the energetic leadership of the Duke of Wellington, Constable from 1826 until 1852. In 1830 the Duke sanctioned one last major attempt to restore the water-filled moat – still a much-valued part of the castle's defences – by means of removing several feet of accumulated silts. The material was conveyed in boxes along a miniature railway and loaded into barges moored near Traitors' Gate bridge, from where it was taken upstream for the use of market gardeners at Battersea. At the same time, measures were taken to improve the perimeter of the moat. In 1829 an old wooden fence that surrounded the top

of the counterscarp – the slope above the top of the moat revetment – was replaced with the existing iron railings, and in 1837 the slope itself was converted into a garden. Despite these endeavours, the problem of the moat returned with a vengeance in 1841. On 4 May *The Times* reported that the garrison had suffered a number of deaths and that eighty men were in hospital as a result of the poor water supply. Two weeks later the Surgeon Major of the Grenadier Guards stationed at the Tower declared that "the bank of filthy mud which is exposed whenever the tide begins to ebb, impregnated with putrid animal and excrementitious matter, surrounded by rank vegetation ... and emitting a most obnoxious smell ... cannot fail to have a most prejudicial effect". After

101. *The Main Guard, a guardhouse created between the White Tower and the Wakefield Tower in 1846, partly within the shell of a seventeenth-century storehouse. Its replacement, built on the same site in 1898–1900, was destroyed in the Second World War (see fig. 102).*

representations from the Tower's medical staff the Duke came to the conclusion that the long-term solution was to convert the moat into a dry ditch or 'fosse'. The Board of Ordnance accepted the Duke's opinion and work began in the spring of 1843. By the end of 1845 the majority of the drainage and infilling work had been completed, rainwater from the Tower now being carried to the river by iron pipes and a giant brick culvert built into the moat fills (fig. 27). The new ground was used for various purposes, including as a parade-ground, although the local feed-merchant's suggestion that he lease the ground for growing mangel-wurzels was politely declined.

By this time work had begun on the building of a vast new barracks for a thousand men on the site of the Grand Storehouse, and on 14 June 1845, amid much ceremony, the Duke of Wellington laid the foundation-stone (fig. 96). Named the Waterloo Barracks to celebrate the Duke's greatest victory, its designer was probably Major Lewis Alexander Hall, who, as head of the London Division of the Royal Engineers, oversaw much of the building work at the Tower from 1840 until his transfer to the Ordnance Survey in 1848. In addition to the Waterloo Barracks, the Royal Engineers provided separate officers' quarters (now the headquarters of the Royal Regiment of Fusiliers) to the north-east of the White Tower (fig. 100), very much in the same style.

Further works were carried out to the curtain wall and towers behind the Waterloo Barracks, which had also been damaged in the fire of 1841: the Brick Tower was converted into an ablutions block for the soldiers in the Waterloo Barracks, while extra accommodation was provided by a new upper floor added to the Bowyer Tower. In 1849 designs were also prepared for a thorough restoration of the Constable Tower, probably as an appendage to the new officers' block.

Within the walls, very considerable works, other than those associated with the Waterloo Barracks and officers' block, were begun in 1846. These were the product of a desire for modernization and improvement that seems to have gripped the Ordnance in the years leading up to its abolition in 1855, but the guiding hand of the Duke of Wellington was never far away. A new main guard was created out of the storehouse erected in 1670–71 to the north of the Wakefield Tower (fig. 101). When the new guard was occupied, the old one, erected in 1717 against the west face of the White Tower, was demolished and the ground level raised and terraced. The year 1846 also saw the demolition of a series of privately owned public houses, the services of which were replaced by military canteens. Two of the best-known inns were the Stone Kitchen and the Golden Chain (fig. 157). The former occupied a range of buildings over the thirteenth-century cross wall and gate immediately west of the Bell Tower, the latter against the west face of the Salt Tower. Demolition of the Golden Chain also included the remaining section of Henry III's south curtain wall and that part of Henry VII's gallery that rested on it.

While works to improve the accommodation of the garrison and to clear the Outer Ward were under way, plans for the last major modernization of the Tower's defences were being prepared. These proposals were a response to the perceived threat of mob attack incited by the widely supported Chartist movement, which, between 1828 and 1858, agitated for an extension of the voting franchise. Encouraged by disturbances in London in 1848, between then and 1852 the authorities saw that the west and north ramparts of the outer wall were cleared of accretions and modified for the improved deployment of artillery and musketry: most of the existing gun emplacements, firing-steps and loopholes date from this time. Subsequently, in 1853, construction of the shell-proof Casemates, to house military stores, workshops and married-mens' quarters, began against the rear of the north wall. Suspended during the Crimean War in 1853–56, when taken up again it included the addition of the massive North Bastion on the exposed angle of the outer curtain wall, mid way between Legge's Mount and Brass Mount (fig. 99): built of brick with a stone facing, and mounting four tiers of guns, this was designed to provide artillery cover over the north moat and the rising ground beyond. Never used in anger, it was destroyed by a German bomb in October 1940 (fig. 176).

A reduction in political tension and lack of funds meant that work on the more dilapidated east wall and its Casemates did not start until 1862, with the building of a high arcaded parapet (best viewed from the ramparts of the eastern inner curtain wall and Tower Bridge approach road), intended to protect troops from any musketry fire from the lofty warehouses of St Katharine Docks to the east, finished in 1852. The last building erected in the nineteenth century for the garrison's use was the Main Guard, a large four-storey structure built in a Jacobean style to the south-west of the White Tower (fig. 102). Constructed of brick and stone between December 1898 and July 1900, it contained, in addition to the guardroom, an orderly room, office and stores, recreation area, mess and lecture rooms. It, too, was destroyed in the Second World War.

102. *The Main Guard, as rebuilt in 1898–1900, to the south-west of the White Tower, shortly after being gutted by fire in October 1940.*

The ROYAL MINT

From its offices and workshops, which are eventually to take up all the Outer Ward, the Tower Mint produces the bulk of England's coinage from the sixteenth to the nineteenth century.

103. Striking coins at the Tower in the early nineteenth century, on the eve of the Mint's departure to new premises, as depicted by Thomas Rowlandson. In the foreground is a coining press, of the kind illustrated in fig. 105, with trays of finished coins or blanks to either side. Others can be seen in operation in the background.

A branch of the Royal Mint – the state organization and workshops responsible for producing the kingdom's coinage – had been permanently established within the secure precincts of the castle under Edward I (see above). But of the day-to-day organization, fortunes and premises of the Tower Mint in the remainder of the Middle Ages we know relatively little, although repairs to Mint buildings are recorded in the fifteenth century. In addition, archaeological excavation has revealed some fascinating traces of its activities in the late fifteenth and early sixteenth centuries in the area of Legge's Mount.

Much more is known about the Mint's activities during and after the reign of Henry VIII (1509–1547). In 1542, for example, one of its tasks was to make coins from silver recently seized from the country's monasteries, closed down by Henry VIII in 1536–40, the urgent demand for cash forcing it, as the French Ambassador noted, "to coin money day and night". Successive reductions of the quantity of precious metal in new coins during the last years of Henry VIII's reign required a recall and re-minting of all the nation's coins (recoinage): the pace and scale of the work this required is illustrated by the story of the artisan William Foxley, who allegedly fell asleep in 1546, at the height of the pressure, and slept for fourteen days and fifteen nights, waking "as if he had slept but one". Under Queen Mary I (1553–1558), as part of her marriage contract with King Philip II of Spain, twenty cartloads of silver were delivered to

the Tower and re-minted into £17,600-worth of English coin. The ordering of another recoinage in the second year of Elizabeth I's reign (1558–1603) initiated a series of building works to provide the necessary space, and between 1560 and 1562 a brick-and-timber building, known as the Upper Mint, was put up at the southern end of the Outer Ward, near the Salt Tower. At the same time, a new refining house (for purifying gold and silver) was constructed at the heart of the old palace area to the south of the White Tower. Further work was carried out in 1566, and in 1585–86 a new administrative office was created, probably on the same site as the surviving eighteenth-century one that stands just north of the Byward Tower (fig. 108).

Machinery was introduced at the Mint in the seventeenth century. Although goldsmiths and coiners – for whom obtaining and measuring the purity of precious metal was essential – had long been at the forefront of metallurgy, the actual methods of coin production had changed little since the Iron Age: a hand-made metal blank was simply placed between engraved dies and struck with a hammer. In 1662, however, screw-operated presses (figs. 103 and 105), first used in Europe in the sixteenth century, were introduced to England. With these, an astonishing twenty to twenty-five coins could be made per minute, although this needed rapid relays of workmen and cost most of the men feeding in the blanks the tips of several fingers. The organization of the Mint was also reviewed, and the Master of

Sir Isaac Newton was appointed Warden of the Tower Mint in 1696 and became Master in 1699, a post he held for 28 years.

A shortage of silver in 1797 forced the government to circulate Spanish dollars, countermarked at the Mint with the head of George III.

The first gold sovereign was minted at the Tower in 1489. It was the largest gold coin that had been struck in England at that time.

104. A coin, the first type to be struck at the Tower of London – a groat (value 4d) of Edward I (left) – and half a guinea (value 10s 6d) of George III, one of the last (right).

the Mint and his employees were, once again (as they had been in the Middle Ages), paid a salary rather than taking a fee for each pound of gold and silver processed.

At the end of the century, another flurry of activity was induced by the recoinage of 1696 – brought on by a massive increase in the illegal practice of shaving off a coin's edges for the metal – and the consequent demands for additional facilities. New space in the Outer Ward could be provided only at the expense of the garrison, who surrendered accommodation in Legge's Mount, together with the barrack block erected in the Irish Mint in the 1680s – leaving the Lieutenant of the Tower complaining that soldiers were having to sleep three in a bed. Elsewhere, new buildings were erected under the supervision of Sir Christopher Wren. We know also that workshops for annealing (softening), blanching (cleaning with acid) and flattening coin blanks were put up in the garden of the Mint Comptroller, between the Constable and

Broad Arrow towers, and that the residence of the Mint Surveyor, on the other side of the castle, was absorbed into the Melting House.

By the end of the eighteenth century the scope for further improvisation was exhausted and the Tower Mint's production capacity, inevitably limited by space, was being outstripped by demand. In 1798 a special committee of the Privy Council established that the Mint should be rehoused outside the castle, and equipped, for the first time, with steam-powered machinery: between 1806 and 1810 a new building, designed in a restrained Palladian style by James Johnson and Robert Smirke, was put up on a site to the north-east. A curious link remained, however, until 1843, in the form of a tunnel to the Tower moat, from which water was drawn for the Mint's use.

The new premises were in use from 1810 until 1978, when the transfer of the operation wholesale to Llantrisant in South Wales was completed.

105. An engraving of 1750 showing a screw-operated coining press and dies. To make a coin, a blank disc of metal was placed on the die (engraved with the coin design in reverse) and pressed against an upper die by turning the screw. A rolling mill, used to produce sheet metal from which the blanks were cut, is shown in operation in the background.

ABOVE 106. *Some of the Tudor metalworking vessels recovered from the excavation of the Mint building in Legge's Mount in 1976.*

ABOVE RIGHT 107. *A nineteenth-century reproduction of a partial plan of the Tower, showing the accommodation used by the Mint in 1701, occupying virtually the whole of the Outer Ward. Coins for England and Ireland were produced in the western and northern arms and the eastern arms respectively. Note the narrowness of the street, particularly at the south-west corner, encroached upon by buildings crammed in on both sides.*

RIGHT 108. *Surviving Mint buildings at the Tower, re-identified in 1992. From drawings prepared before and after 1800 they can be identified (south to north) as the Mint Office, Assay Office, coal houses and Moulding and Melting House.*

The Tower
RECORD OFFICE

From the late seventeenth century new systems emerge
for the storage and cataloguing of state records, left in a
"deplorable pickle" after the Civil War.

LEFT 109. *The upper chamber
in the Wakefield Tower in 1801,
showing the panelling and
cupboards fitted early in the
previous century. Watercolour
by Charles Tomkins.*

BELOW 110. *Book plate used
by the Tower Record Office,
c. 1760.*

Even medieval government produced a vast volume of documents, including the official records of orders issued to the provinces, grants of lands and property, diplomatic papers and much else. Copies of a lot of this material had to be kept for future reference, for example by government officials and lawyers in pursuit of legal precedent and property disputes. This led to the establishment of an administrative machinery for the management of records, partly controlled, from the thirteenth century onwards, by the Master of the Rolls (so called because most records were kept on sheets of parchment or paper rolled up for storage). The records also required secure storage, and for reasons of convenience many were kept at Westminster Abbey, close to the royal palace and the courts. Others repositories also existed, including, from the late fourteenth century, that of the Chancery records (royal letters and related material) in Chancery Lane – later, from 1858 until 1996, the site of the Public Record Office (see p. 89). However, as London's greatest stronghold, and still conveniently close to Westminster, it is not surprising that from at least the late thirteenth century the Tower of London also sheltered a major repository.

Important though the records were, purpose-built accommodation at the Tower was never provided, and they were stored in various parts of the royal lodgings, vying for space with other Tower-based organizations, the Ordnance in particular. In 1360, for example, records were held in the White Tower, although removed in that year to make room for the captured King of France, Jean le Bon, imprisoned there between 1359 and 1361. In the later Middle Ages the main repository was in the Wakefield Tower, but by the reign of James I (1603–1625) the White Tower was again in use. Given the inherent inconvenience of storage in the White Tower, and that the records now shared it with hundreds of tons of gunpowder, this was not ideal: it was vainly recommended in 1620 that the powder should be removed, an issue raised again, with an equal lack of success, in 1718 and 1832. Documents concerning another accommodation problem of the period – a dispute with the Ordnance over the occupation of a building attached to the east side of the Wakefield Tower – give an interesting glimpse of the working conditions this unstable situation could lead to. In 1662 the Keeper of the Records, William Prynne, claimed that without the extra space his staff had no fire at hand to warm themselves, and were greatly hindered in sorting, transcribing and making tables of records. Within these improvised premises, storage conditions, too, were rarely satisfactory. Although an exceptional piece of furniture was made in 1622–23 "to putt the auntient Bills of Parliament therein", a generation later the situation was again in need of improvement. When William Prynne took over the office of Keeper in 1660, he reported that the records at the Tower were in "a deplorable pickle ... overspread with dust and cobwebs and eaten up with

LEFT William Prynne, Keeper of Tower Records to Charles II, had his ears cut off by Charles I for seditious writings.

RIGHT When the Keeper of the Records, William Lambarde, presented his digest of the records to Elizabeth I, she said nothing had brought "so great delectation to her" since her accession.

During the Interregnum the records of Scotland had been brought to the Tower, but many of them were lost when one of the ships taking them back in 1660 sank in bad weather.

rust, cankers, moths, worms, in their over-much neglected cells". He later wrote that "I have at last tumbled them all over, and distributed them into sundry indigested heaps, which I intend God willing to reduce into order by degrees". The task, however, was too much for him, and his successor as Keeper, Sir Algernon May, found the condition of the records in "Cesars Chappell" (*i.e.* the White Tower chapel) deplorable, the presses being "broke down & burnt by the Soldiers who did lye there and Rolles and whatever they were of several natures thrown into one heap contayneing diverse cart Loads all mingled promiscuously togeather", probably the result of vandalism during the Interregnum. Again, in 1704 a Committee of the House of Lords found the records in the chapel lying "in a confused heap" on a broken floor. But this time proper shelves and presses were then installed, transforming it, by 1707, into what a Committee of Inspection described as a "noble repository". Further improvements were made a few years later to the upper chamber of the Wakefield Tower and part of the medieval chamber-block to the east, which included fine panelling to the walls,

"framed into presses round the rooms wherein which are shelves and repositories for the reception of records". Openings for sash windows were punched through the medieval curtain wall to let in more light, and the Record Office's main entrance, opening into the Outer Ward immediately beside the Wakefield Tower, was given an elaborate stone surround and surmounted with the royal coat of arms (fig. 113): it was this building that was to be swept away amid such controversy in the 1880s (see p. 121). More space was gained in 1736, when, after more than twenty years of intermittent negotiations with the Ordnance, an additional room in the White Tower (on the north side of the chapel on the top floor) was finally secured. A near disaster in 1788, when the Ordnance Office next to the Wakefield Tower burnt down, led the Keeper, Thomas Astle, to fireproof the upper Wakefield repository with iron shutters and an iron ceiling, but no actual expansion of the premises was allowed until 1808, when the two rooms at the top of the north-east turret were made available, followed three years later by all the rooms on the two upper floors, newly provided with

111. A view by Frederick Nash of c. 1810 showing the Chapel of St John the Evangelist in the White Tower in use as a records store, looking across the nave. Rolled documents are housed in presses, probably those installed in 1704–07.

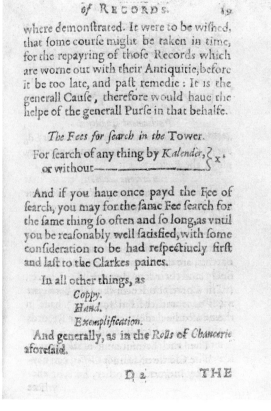

ABOVE 112. *A page from a* Direction for Search of Records, *published by Thomas Powell, a member of the Record Office staff, in 1622. The fee of 10 shillings for helping the reader to find what they were looking for seems exorbitant, but the amount of assistance which could be expected seems to have been fairly generous.*

113. *View by Charles Tomkins of about 1800 showing the Wakefield Tower with the seventeenth-century entrance to the Record Office, adorned with the royal arms, immediately beside it. The office and its entrance were destroyed when the surrounding wall, part of the medieval inner curtain, was incorrectly realigned in 1885 (see p. 121).*

the collections at the Tower but also those at Westminster and Chancery Lane (fig. 112). This also set out the charges that, until salaries were introduced in 1651, provided the staff with their only payment: the charge for the search of a document was 1s, for producing a document 4d, and for copying 8d per sheet. Salaries did not stop fees being exacted from readers, however, and at a rate that some considered extortionate. In 1830, for example, the antiquary Sir Nicholas Harris Nicolas complained that, at the Tower, "no individual can inspect a document which is confessedly the property of the public, and for which the public is taxed, without paying the sum of 16s 8d, of which 10s is for making the search, as it is termed, and six shillings and eight pence for one of the clerks rising from his chair, walking a few yards and opening a roll".

Nevertheless, the Tower Record Office staff were also charged with the serious task of producing indexes and lists of documents, and means of storing them to ease their use and retrieval. The first known instance of this had been at Westminster in the 1290s, when a range of documents were classified and marked with pictograms identifying their subject-matter, while the first known effort of this kind at the Tower was made in the 1320s. But the process of cataloguing and listing the Tower records in anything like the modern sense began in the second half of the sixteenth century with the Keeper, Thomas Bowyer, who spent eight years producing a six-volume summary of the records, and his successor, William Lambarde. In the seventeenth and eighteenth centuries major advances were made under scholarly keepers such Astle and the famous antiquary Samuel Lysons, the latter in office from 1804 to his death in 1819.

The major users of the records and their indexes and calendars throughout the period concerned were lawyers, but, from the seventeenth century onwards, as historians moved from using chronicles to documents, they began to be used for historical research. Much important work, and the transcription for publication of various categories of documents, was carried out at the Tower Record Office, and great historians of the seventeenth, eighteenth and nineteenth centuries, such as Thomas Rymer, Anthony à Wood and Sir William Dugdale, all worked there at one time or another.

skylights. But by then the days of the Tower Record Office were numbered. As early as 1800 a Select Committee of the House of Commons had recommended that the manuscripts from the numerous record repositories in and around London, including the Tower's, be concentrated in one building. After years of debate and inaction, the principle was enshrined in the Public Records Act of 1838, which re-centralized control under the Master of the Rolls and a Deputy Keeper. Work on the building of the central repository in Chancery Lane began in 1851, though the Tower remained a 'branch office' until the new building opened in 1858. In the 1970s new premises were built at Kew, to which most original records had been transferred by 1996.

Arrangements for supplying records from the Tower of London for their use at the Tower office must always have existed, but are known about in some detail from the seventeenth century onwards. The first guide to the records was prepared by the Keeper, William Lambarde, who presented them to Queen Elizabeth I in 1601. In 1622 Thomas Powell published his *Direction for Search of Records*, covering

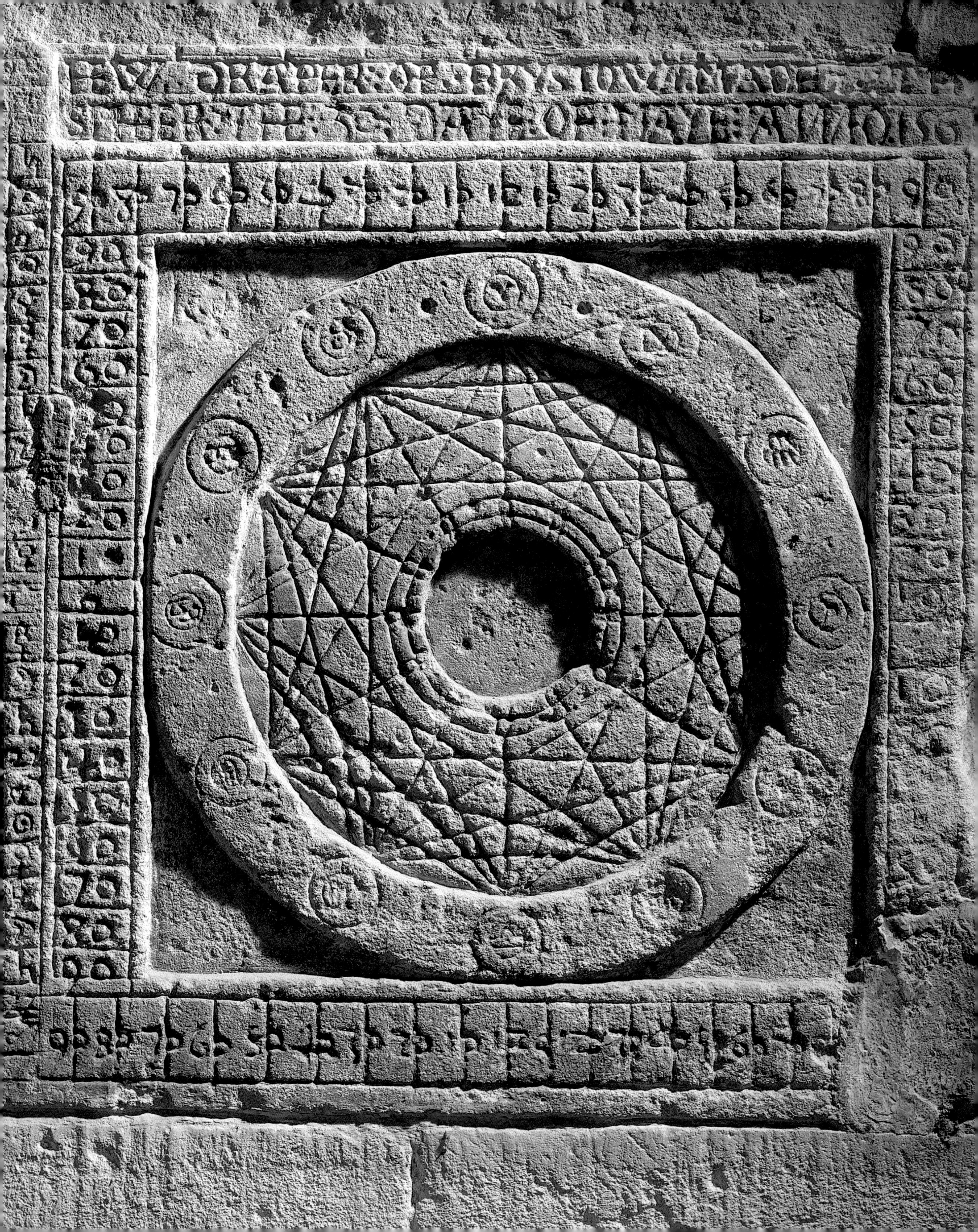

The STATE PRISON

Regularly used as a prison from its earliest days to the 1820s, the Tower holds its highest concentration of prisoners in the sixteenth century; some live in comfort, others escape, a few are tortured or executed.

114. Carving and inscription in the Salt Tower by Hugh Draper of Bristol, imprisoned there in 1561 on charges of sorcery.

One of the best-known roles of the Tower is that of a place of imprisonment, torture and execution, largely as a result of propagandist accounts by religious extremists in the sixteenth century and the myth-makers of the nineteenth, particularly Harrison Ainsworth. The lovingly invented account in Ainsworth's *The Tower of London: A Historical Romance* of a subterranean torture-chamber, its horrific equipment, and the "open volume in which were taken down the confessions of the sufferers", stuck firmly in the popular imagination. But the reality, although no less interesting, was rather different. The Tower's role as a prison, as with that of all castles, was only incidental to its main functions, although in this case its importance was enhanced by its own status and its proximity to the royal courts at Westminster, which made it a convenient holding-place for prisoners of rank and importance. It served as such from at least the imprisonment of its first known prisoner, Ranulf Flambard, in 1100, until 1820 (apart from exceptional use in the twentieth century; see p. 123), but even when the prisoner population was at its height during the religious and political upheavals of the sixteenth and seventeenth centuries, imprisonment played only a minor part in the castle's daily life.

The incidental nature of the Tower's role as a prison is underlined by the absence of almost any purpose-built accommodation, the exception being the 'Prison for Soldiers' – a brick shed – built against the rear of the Main Guard, to the north-west of the White Tower, in 1687. As a result, prisoners had to be accommodated in whatever space was available. High-ranking prisoners in the Middle Ages were simply secured in some part of the royal or other lodgings. Anne Boleyn, for example, executed at the Tower in 1536, was lodged in part of the old palace, as was the young Princess Elizabeth (the future Elizabeth I). Areas outside normal or even previous domestic use were also pressed into service, such as the newly erected Long House of Ordnance, in which Dr Tunstal, late Bishop of Durham, was confined in 1552. Some deliberate rationalization of prisoner accommodation, however, followed the arrival of Sir William Waad as Lieutenant of the Tower in 1605, and alterations were made to the Bloody Tower for the celebrated adventurer, explorer and author Sir Walter Ralegh, held at the Tower until 1618. The extensive rebuilding carried out by the Board of Ordnance after the Restoration in 1660 (see pp. 61–71), and the consequent loss of prison space, led to more reorganization. The problem was again addressed at the end of the century – Sir Christopher Wren, Surveyor General of the King's Works, being instructed in 1695 to prepare an estimate for converting the rooms in the Beauchamp and Bloody towers into prison lodgings and to design a prison (unexecuted) to be built behind the Chapel of St Peter ad Vincula.

Conditions of confinement at the Tower during most of its history took two main forms: close con-

Sir Thomas Wyatt (imprisoned 1554) led a rebellion against Queen Mary. The fighting at Charing Cross could be heard from the roof of the White Tower.

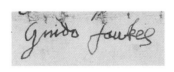

Guy Fawkes was brought to the Tower on 6 November 1605; only after ten days of interrogation, and probably torture, did he give a full confession.

In 1599 Father John Gerard escaped from the Cradle Tower. He later told how he used orange juice as invisible ink to communicate with his friends.

RIGHT 115. *Sir Thomas More, one of the Tower's most famous prisoners, held there from 1534 until his execution a year later. Portrait of 1527 after Hans Holbein.*

FAR RIGHT 116. *Portrait of Sir Walter Ralegh, attributed to the monogrammist 'H', dated 1588. A brilliant soldier, adventurer, and favourite of Elizabeth I, Ralegh fell from favour in 1591, was accused of treason under James I in 1603 and spent much of the next fifteen years imprisoned in the Tower.*

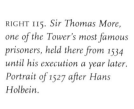

117. *Marginal illustration by Matthew Paris in his* Greater Chronicle, *showing the Welsh Prince Gruffydd ap Llewelyn falling to his death while escaping from the Tower in 1244.*

finement, whereby the prisoner was secured in his quarters and subject to strictly regulated security, and confinement simply within the castle precincts. In the Middle Ages their needs and security were entrusted to a gaoler, appointed by the Constable, but under Henry VIII the duty was devolved to the Yeoman Warders, one of whom took charge as Gentleman Gaoler (a post, albeit now an honorary one, that still exists). Most prisoners' actual conditions at the Tower were not necessarily as grim as usually supposed, even the most lowly individuals being better off than in a crowded public prison such as the Fleet, where death from disease was at times a near certainty. For the more exalted prisoner, material conditions could even be quite comfortable: the widow of the Protector Somerset, for example, imprisoned in 1551, enjoyed as lavish a table as she might have done at home and the attentions of at least four servants. A list of possessions that the Privy Council agreed to send to the imprisoned Earl of Castlehaven in 1630 included luxurious items such as a "bed of crimson taffeta", "12 peeces of tapestry neare suitable as they may bee" and "three turkie carpets", in addition to bedding for a servant. Prisoners' accommodation could also be physically adapted to their requirements, or, as it was for Ralegh – whose son Carew was born at the Tower in 1605 – to house members of their family. But most prisoners suffered, of course, from depression and boredom, to which we owe many of the painstakingly carved inscriptions in the Salt and Beauchamp towers and elsewhere (fig. 114).

Given the *ad hoc* nature of their accommodation

and the occasional laxity of the régime, it is not surprising that there were many successful escapes – starting, of course, with Ranulf Flambard – although there were failures, too. Celebrated escapees in the post-medieval period have included the Jesuit John Gerard (see below), Mrs Alice Tankerville – who temporarily regained her freedom with the help of her guard in 1534 – and the Jacobite Lord Nithsdale, who made his escape, dressed in his wife's clothes, in 1716 (fig. 153).

Although the incidence of torture and execution at the Tower has been exaggerated, such punishments did indeed await an unfortunate few. Horrible as it was, the fact that in England torture could be ordered only by the Privy Council meant that its use was extremely rare, no more than forty-eight cases receiving official sanction, for example, between 1540 and 1640. There were three main methods, the most common form being the rack (fig. 120), last used in 1640: although kept in readiness as late as 1673, by July 1675 it had clearly been decommissioned, for in that month it makes its first appearance as "the rack of torment" among a number of other curiosities in the Ordnance inventories. The second infamous device was the 'Scavenger's daughter', a set of leg, wrist and neck irons, which forced the victim into bone-crushing contortions (figs. 120 and 122). Equally foul, although simpler, were the 'manacles', by which the prisoner was suspended by the wrists – an experience vividly described by one of its victims, the Jesuit priest Father Gerard, after his eventual escape. When it came to execution, the Tower was usually no more than the point of departure for prisoners led off to

LEFT 118. *The upper room of Ralegh's lodging in the Bloody Tower, originally inserted in 1605–06 to provide extra space for his family and attendants (shown as rebuilt in 1974).*

BELOW 119. *The block and axe, which have been displayed together at the Tower since the middle of the nineteenth century. Similar equipment was undoubtedly used to behead most of the seven prisoners executed in the castle, although the provenance of these particular items is uncertain.*

BOTTOM 120. *A plate from John Foxe's* Acts and Monuments, *or 'Book of Martyrs', of 1563, showing the Protestant deacon Cuthbert Simpson being tortured on the rack in the reign of the Catholic Queen Mary. Inset are illustrations and descriptions of other torments to which he was subjected.*

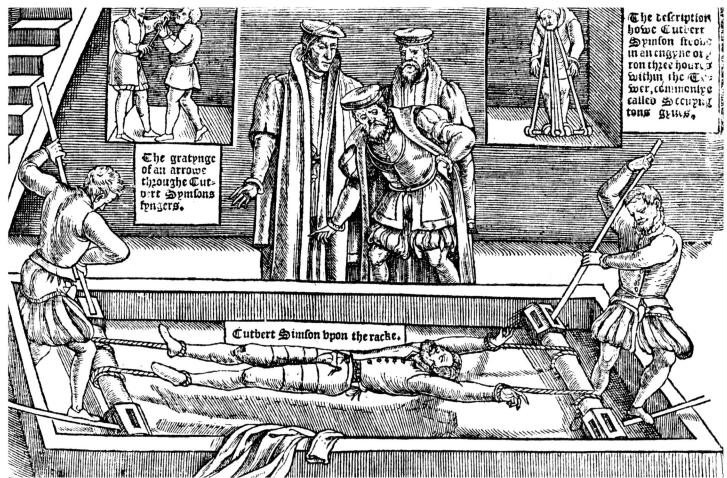

121. *The execution of the rebel Scottish peers Balmerino and Kilmarnock on Tower Hill in 1746, almost the last to take place there. Note the vast size of the crowd and the improvised viewing stands along the edge of the moat.*

execution elsewhere, usually at Tyburn (near Marble Arch), or, closer to home, Tower Hill – a total of 112 of them over 400 years. Tower officials were, however, directly involved when executions took place within the walls, a dubious privilege accorded to particularly high-ranking individuals, or when, as in the case of Lady Jane Grey or the Earl of Essex

(executed in 1554 and 1601 respectively), popular sympathy would have made public execution too dangerous. Contrary to what today's visitor may imagine or be told, only seven such events took place, although there were later to be a handful of executions during the two world wars of the twentieth century (see p. 123).

The PUBLIC SHOWPLACE

The Tower, always a spectacle in itself, attracts further attention when its royal storehouses – the Jewel House and Armouries, together with the Menagerie – begin to be enhanced for public view in the sixteenth century.

LEFT 122. *Illustration from a guide to the Tower of about 1820, showing three of its attractions: weaponry and instruments of torture, the Line of Kings and the Menagerie.*

RIGHT 123. *The western approach to the Tower viewed from near the Middle Tower in 1934. The long single-storey building with the overhanging eaves, built in 1851, was the Tower's first purpose-built ticket office, with lavatories and a refreshment-room incorporated.*

Visiting the Tower

The Tower was always intended as a showpiece and symbol of power and authority, and must always have been sought out by, or shown to, London's visitors – whether foreign dignitaries or ordinary Englishmen. But by Tudor times its appeal was already taking on another dimension, based not just on its appearance, but its associations with many of the great events and personalities of history. In addition, in the sixteenth and seventeenth centuries there was a growing interest in the assembling and viewing of collections of curiosities, with which the Tower was uniquely well provided, thanks to its function as a gigantic official warehouse. Moreover, the working institutions of the Tower were seen as attractions in their own right.

That deliberate practice of showing the sights of the Tower to visitors was well established by the middle of Elizabeth I's reign (1558–1603), as indicated by the Privy Council's order to the Lieutenant and officers of the Armoury and Ordnance in 1578 to show a certain Monsieur Kentall, a gentleman from High Germany, the castle and "suche thinges as are usuallie showed therein". Whereas Kentall was shown the Tower at the request of the highest authorities – no doubt in the hope of impressing him with the size and contents of the arsenal – other visitors were by then going to the Tower on their own initiative. Early visitors sometimes refer to having gained permission to view the fortress in advance of their visit, but by the middle of the next century it seems they simply presented themselves at the gate and, having surrendered any arms they were carrying, were taken round the fortress by a Yeoman Warder guide. Such ease of access to a major military headquarters was perhaps unusual by European standards: certainly it impressed Sophia von La Roche, who noted in 1786 that such easy "entrance into the Tower should endear his motherland to every Englishman ... This seems to me the most outstanding difference between London and Paris; the foreigner is shown the Tower, while he dare not even look at the Bastille."

The cost of viewing the Tower's attractions during the late Tudor and Stuart periods seems to have varied in accordance with the status of the visitor, but could be extraordinarily high. For example, when Thomas

Thomas Cromwell, Henry VIII's chief minister, was appointed Master of the Jewels in 1532; under his supervision the jewel houses in the Tower were rebuilt.

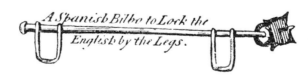

The 'Spanish Armoury' – supposed to have contained spoils from the Armada – was described in the early nineteenth century as "the last stronghold of humbug" at the Tower.

On 26 January 1885 a bomb exploded in the White Tower, severely damaging hundreds of rifles on display.

124. *Detail of a model of the Grand Storehouse, showing the giant 'organ' flanked by a serpent and a seven-headed monster at the east end of the Small Armoury.*

teenth century the cost of viewing the combined Armouries was regularized at 3 shillings per person, and in 1838 this was cut to 1 shilling, lowered to 6 pence in the following year, a figure that was maintained for the rest of the century, although admission to the Menagerie or the Jewel House was extra. The effect of price reduction between 1837 and 1839 was a rise in visitor numbers from 10,500 to 80,000 per annum. By the end of the nineteenth century, and with the introduction in 1875 of free admission on Mondays, Saturdays and official holidays, visitors numbered more than half a million.

The main sights of the Tower during most of this period were the Armouries, Ordnance stores and displays, the Menagerie, the Wardrobe and the Jewel House (fig. 122). During the nineteenth century the castle itself came to be recognized as perhaps the greatest sight of all – both a cause and a result of the vast programme of 're-medievalization' between the 1850s and the 1880s (see pp. 117–21).

The Armouries

Weaponry of various sorts must always have been on view and shown to the Tower's visitors, but by the end of the sixteenth century they were already being shown items selected for their historical interest. In 1592, for example, Jacob Rathgeb, secretary to Frederick, Duke of Württemberg, describes how he and the Duke were shown historic arms, including a musket that belonged to Henry VIII and a gigantic lance, clearly that – still on display at the Tower – traditionally associated with his brother-in-law, Charles Brandon, Duke of Suffolk. In 1598 another German visitor, Paul Hentzner, recorded being shown many items belonging to Henry VIII, including a gilt suit of armour and several historic cannon, among the latter being two wooden pieces deployed to deceive the French at the Siege of Boulogne in 1544.

Unfavourable comparison by Rathgeb between the Tower displays and those in Germany and his complaint that they are "full of dust and stand about in the greatest confusion and disorder", suggest that little attention was then being paid to presentation. In the second half of the seventeenth century, however, the situation changed with the creation of four displays specifically designed for the public. The first, the Spanish Armoury, was an assemblage of fearsome-looking weapons and a few instruments of torture, claimed to have been taken from the Armada of 1588, and with which the Spaniards had supposedly been intending to torment the conquered English. Although few, if any, of the items had any Spanish connections, and others are known to have been at the Tower since the reign of Henry VIII (1509–1547), the Spanish Armoury served its main purpose – condemning the Spaniards and intimating English invincibility. Installed in the old Long

Platter visited the fortress in 1599 he made eight payments at different locations, the first, of 3 shillings, being in one of the armouries in the White Tower to "a keeper in attendance". Lady Judith Barrington gave away 11 shillings in largesse when she visited the fortress in the autumn of 1639, while General Patrick Gordon's collective payments amounted to no less than 33 shillings in 1660 – enough to pay the wages of a workman for four months. By 1693, however, a French guide to London was instructing its readers on the value of gratuities to be presented at different locations in the fortress, and by 1729 the cost of viewing the Mint, Jewel House, Menagerie and Armouries had been fixed, with prices being printed in English and French in the *Foreigner's Guide to London and Westminster*. Similar prices are quoted in the first complete guide to the Tower of London, which appeared twelve years later. Impecunious-looking visitors could still, however, be treated in a less than respectful manner: William Hutton attempted to enter the Tower in 1749, but, as he relates in his book *A Journey from Birmingham to London*, "my Derbyshire dialect quickly brought the warders out of their lodges; who on seeing the dust about my shoes, wisely concluded that money could not abound in my pocket, and, with the voice of authority, ordered me back".

It was only in the early nineteenth century, however, that special arrangements began to be made for accommodating visitors: in 1838 a ticket office was created out of three old animals' cages at the western entrance, where visitors could buy refreshments and an official guidebook. Thirteen years later this was replaced by a purpose-built office with lavatories attached (fig. 123). Despite the antipathy of the Duke of Wellington, who proposed that, for military reasons, the Tower should be closed to visitors, they continued to be encouraged with better facilities and successive price reductions. During the first years of the nine-

TOP 125. The 'Line of Kings' as depicted by Thomas Rowlandson in 1809, when still housed in the New Armouries building.

ABOVE 126. View of the Small Armoury on the first floor of the Grand Storehouse in 1822. Note the columns, pilasters and other features made up of or festooned with weapons.

127. Late nineteenth-century photograph showing the mounted figure of Elizabeth I and her page, commemorating her address to the English forces at Tilbury in August 1588, about to engage the Spanish Armada. The tableau was made for inclusion in the seventeenth-century 'Spanish Armoury' when war broke out with Spain in 1779, clearly to reinforce the message of English invincibility and Spanish perfidy which was the aim of the whole display. In 1837 the display was moved to the crypt of the White Tower chapel, where it is shown in this photograph.

House of Ordnance to the north of the White Tower (fig. 70) until its demolition in 1688, the Spanish Armoury was then redisplayed on the first floor of a storehouse erected immediately north of the Wakefield Tower in 1670–71. While there, it was enhanced, at the outbreak of war with Spain in 1779, with an equestrian figure of Elizabeth I addressing the English forces at Tilbury. In 1837 the display – by then renamed Queen Elizabeth's Armoury – was moved to the crypt of the White Tower chapel.

The second display – the Line of Kings – was, as the name suggests, a row of figures representing the kings of England, mounted on life-size wooden horses. The line is first recorded in the Tower in an inventory dated October 1660, in which the figures are described as "standing formerly at Greenwich in the Green Gallery", and thus may have included some or all of a group of eight horses recorded there in Henry VIII's inventory of 1547. The line was extended in 1685 with the addition of a horse and effigy of Charles II and one of Charles I in the following year, both the work of Grinling Gibbons. Originally also displayed in the House of Ordnance, the line was rehoused in 1688 on the first floor of the New Armouries building to the south-east of the White Tower and enlarged and enhanced by seventeen new horses. A dummy of William III was added in 1702, and George I belatedly joined him in 1750, represented by a bronze head made by the sculptor John Cheere. The final figure, that of George II, was added in 1768. In 1825 the Line of Kings moved once again, this time to a purpose-built structure, the New Horse Armoury, up against the south face of the White Tower. At the same time it was rearranged by Dr Samuel Meyrick, the first serious scholar of arms and armour, in a more scientific, if less picturesque manner (fig. 125) – depriving William the Conqueror, for example, of his musket. Although one of the earliest purpose-built museums in the country, and the first neo-Gothic building at the Tower – intended to harmonize with the White Tower – it was much

128. The interior of the Grand Storehouse on the morning after the fire of 1841, showing the smouldering remains of its larger exhibits.

RIGHT 129. *A sixteenth-century multi-barrelled bronze cannon, once on display in the Grand Storehouse, and partially melted by the fire that destroyed it.*

BELOW 130. *The last hours of the Grand Storehouse on the night of 30 October 1841, by William Smith. Note the massed crowds in the foreground, and the new Royal Mint of 1810–12 on the left, lit up by the flames.*

BOTTOM 131. *Engraving of the west room on the top floor of the White Tower in 1863, showing the display of thousands of rifles on show between 1863 and 1883. At this time the intention was still to impress rather than to offer the visitor any serious instruction.*

despised: Thomas Allen, in his *History and Antiquities of London* published in 1827, regretted "that the Government should have allowed a paltry building like that of the New Horse Armoury to have been erected against the venerable and noble White Tower", while a commentator writing in *The Builder* in July 1851 thought the "perpetrator" of the design "deserved to be beheaded". Both Queen Elizabeth's Armoury and the Line of Kings continued to be altered until their contents were dispersed among the various displays in the upper floors of the White Tower in the early 1880s.

The third, and most spectacular, armoury to be formed at the Tower was installed on the first floor of the Grand Storehouse, shortly after its construction in 1688–92. This was the Small Armoury – so called as it was composed of small arms rather than artillery – an incredible tableau composed of tens of thousands of weapons, and a mass of elaborate wooden carvings, set up under the direction of one John Harris of Eaton in 1696. Among the many creations composed of frames dressed with weapons were an "organ", its large pipes made out of brass blunderbusses, its smaller ones by two thousand pistols, a "fiery serpent" and a "seven-headed monster". It was, according to the eighteenth-century antiquarian William Maitland, a sight "no one ever beheld without Astonishment ... not to be matched perhaps in the world". Although Harris's displays were completely destroyed in the fire of 1841, an impression of the effect may be gained at Hampton Court Palace, where a more solemn arrangement by the same hand still survives, and in the White Tower, where a re-created section has been included in the new displays.

The fourth armoury on view to the public, known as the Artillery Room, displayed the great guns of the "Train" of Artillery – the endless column of cannon and ammunition wagons that followed the army in the field. In the early years most of these guns could have been used, but as time went by the room increasingly took on the appearance of a museum of British military might, as cannon and other trophies captured from battlefields around the world were brought here to be displayed. Other, more indigenous curiosities were also on show: Edward Hatton, in his *New View of London* of 1708, notes the presence of a brass gun made for James I's eldest son, Prince Henry, the infamous (and long-since decommissioned) "Rack to extort Confession", and Henry VIII's wooden cannon. Although the Train of Artillery had been moved to Greenwich Arsenal a few years before, most of the remaining exhibits were damaged or destroyed in the fire of 1841 (fig. 128).

The Menagerie

By the end of the Middle Ages the Menagerie at the Tower was located, as it appears to have been since at least the reign of Edward III, in the Lion Tower at

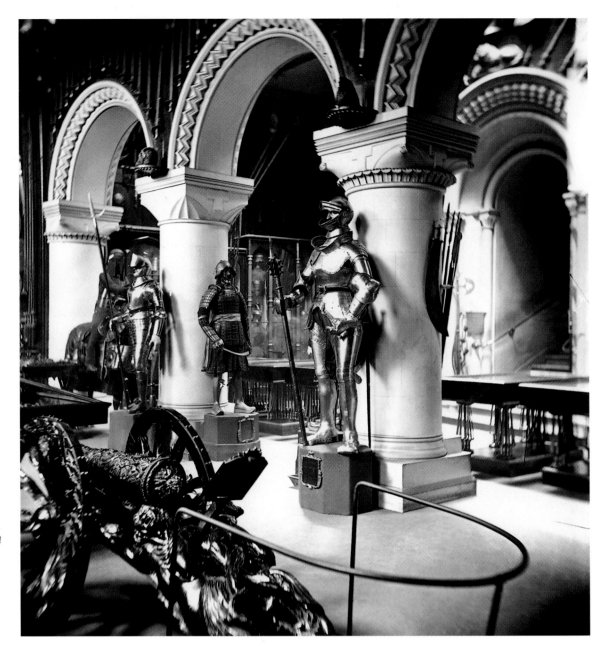

132. *The vestibule at the east end of the New Horse Armoury in about 1870. Visitors could reach the Spanish Armoury in the crypt of the White Tower via the staircase behind the imitated Norman columns. The vestibule housed the earliest displays of Oriental arms and armour at the Tower, most of the objects being trophies captured during the Opium War with China in 1840–42.*

the western entrance (see p. 36). Originally for the amusement of the king and his associates, the Menagerie became a public attraction during the reign of Elizabeth I. In 1598 Hentzner, one of the first visitors to leave his impressions, recorded seeing "three Lionesses, one Lion of great size ... a Tyger, a Lynx; a Wolf ... Porqupine, and an Eagle", noting that they were "kept in a remote place, fitted up for the purpose with lattices at the Queen's expense". Under James I the collection of animals was enlarged, while the facilities in and about the Lion Tower were extended and improved. Between 1604 and 1606 the existing two-storey cages against the inside face of the tower were extensively refurbished. Floors were relaid, with those in the upper level being fitted with channels to take away the lions' urine, new stairs installed to allow the animals to climb from one level to another, and the pulley-operated cage doors repaired. An exercise yard

was created in part of the moat around the Lion Tower, now drained and dammed off from the Thames by a brick wall (fig. 135). Within the yard masons constructed a "great cisterne ... for the Lyons to drincke and washe themselfes in". Two passageways were forced through the "thicke round wall" of the Lion Tower to provide access from the dens, closed by sliding doors operated by pulleys; overhead, a great viewing platform was erected for "the kinges Matie to stande on". These improvements were also recorded by the chronicler Edmond Howes, who notes that part of the new yard was intended for a lioness named Elizabeth, who whelped in August 1604 and again in February 1605, while the main exercise yard could also be used to "baight the Lyons with dogges, beares, bulles, bores, etc" for the amusement of the king.

The Menagerie seems to have continued to flourish during the Interregnum, James Howel noting in the

1650s that the Tower was never "better furnished with lions than it is now, there being six in all, young and old". Shortly after the Restoration, the Dutch artist William Schellinks visited the Tower and was shown six lions, one kept with a dog as companion – a phenomenon often described by later visitors – a lioness, two leopards and two eagles. Further improvements soon followed, and in July 1671 contracts were signed to erect a new two-storey residence for the Menagerie Keeper, William Gill, in the tower "where the Kings Lyons be kept", and between 1672 and 1675 a new 'Lion House' was put up in the south-east corner of the Lion Tower. Subsequently, in 1733, the Keeper, John Martin, petitioned the King to have the house enlarged, and during the following year plans were approved to build an additional third storey.

By the 1720s surveys indicate that buildings had been constructed in the exercise yard, and it was probably here that some of the increasing number of exotic animals were housed. Strype, in his edition of *Stow's London*, lists the following animals at the Tower in June 1704: six lions, two leopards or tigers, three eagles, two Swedish owls "of great bigness", two "Cats of the Mountains" and a jackal. He also notes the presence of two stuffed lions, one of them having belonged to Charles II ("now in much decay"), and the other to Queen Mary II.

In the first true guidebook to the Tower, published in 1741, the animals listed include the lions Marco and Phillis and their son Nero, two lionesses called Jenny and Nanny, three lion cubs, a leopard called Will, a panther called Jenny, two tigers called Will and Phillis and their son Dick, a racoon, two vultures, two eagles, a porcupine, an ape and a strange bird from the East Indies called a 'warwoven' (fig. 133). Later in the century the guides refer to the "School of Monkeys" as one of the principal attractions (fig. 134). The fact that visitors were allowed to enter the room without a barrier between them and the animals may have resulted in an incident that brought about the closure of the "school", for in 1810 a guidebook informed its readers that "formerly several monkies were kept, but one of them having torn a boy's leg in a dangerous manner they were removed".

BELOW LEFT 133. *Illustrations from* Curiosities in the Tower of London, *a miniature children's guidebook published in 1741, showing animals in the Menagerie.*

BELOW RIGHT 134. *The School of Monkeys, a cartoon published by Thomas Rowlandson, showing one of the spectacles offered to Menagerie visitors in the late eighteenth century.*

BOTTOM RIGHT 135. *The Lions' den in 1779, showing the two-storey cages that, in one form or another, had occupied the semicircular Lion Tower since at least the sixteenth century.*

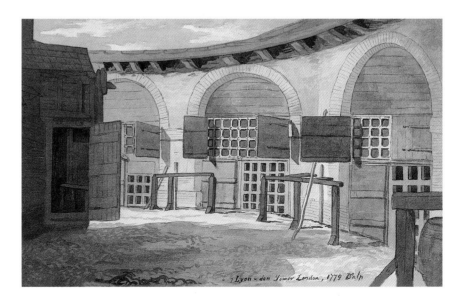

THE
KING'S MENAGERIE
ROYAL,
TOWER OF LONDON.

THIS ANCIENT EDIFICE,
Built in the Reign of Edward IV. in the year 1465.
FOR THE RECEPTION OF
Foreign Beast, Birds, &c.

PRESENTED TO THE KINGS OF ENGLAND,
Could never, since its foundation, boast of a more magnificent or splendid VARIETY than it does at present.

The Nobility, Gentry and Public, are most respectfully informed, that Mr COPS has imported the greatest collection of REPTILES ever before seen in Europe, viz:—

Great Boa Constrictor Serpent
from Ceylon.—Also the Wonder of the Age, never before seen alive in England,
The Harlequin Snake,
Where variety of brilliant Colours and great Beauty, surpasses the possibility of description.
The Rattle Snake,
from North America.
A Rock Serpent,
from Bengal.
Anaconda Serpents,
from the Island of Java.
A Crocodile,
From the River Nile.
Two beautiful Chamelions,
from Africa.
A beautiful Zebra,
from Ethiopia.
Pair of Kangaroos,
(Male and Female). Bred in Windsor Great Park.
A Kangaroo Rat,
(The smallest of that species), from Botany Bay.
A remarkably beautiful Ocelot
Or, Tiger in Miniature.
The Civet Cat,
(The Animal that produces Musk), from China.
The Mouflon,
from Caffraria.

Four Emews,
Or Southern Ostriches.
A Pelican of the Wilderness,
An extraordinary Bird, represented to feed the Young with its own Blood.
Ardea Dubia,
Or, Adjutant of Bengal, commonly called the Gigantic Crane.
Three Belearic or Royal Crowned Cranes.
Pair of Black Swans,
from Van Diemen's Land.
A beautiful Golden Vulture,
from Demerara.
The majestic Eagle of the Sun,
from North America.
Pair of beautiful Horned Owls
from Hudson's Bay.
Pair of Storks,
from Ethiopia.
Two pair of Curacoa Birds,
from Trinidad.

Chinese Gold and Silver Pheasants, Macaws, Cockatoos, Parrots, Paroquets, and a great variety of other Birds of most splendid plumage.

SECOND DIVISION.

A full grown majestic Silver Maned Lion and his Consort,
In one Den, being the largest that has been brought to England for many years, and presented to the King by General Watson: the only pair of this kind ever seen in England.

Pair of beautiful Young Lions
from the Cape of Good Hope.

Pr. handsome hunting Leopards
from Seringapatam.
Pair enormous Black Wolves,
from the Polar Regions: the only ones ever seen alive in England.
The Bradypus Pentadactylis,
Or, Five Fingered Sloth.—The greatest curiosity the Menagerie ever held, as it is the first (after repeated efforts) ever brought alive to this Country.

THIRD DIVISION.

Three African Blood Hounds and the Sashe,
Very extraordinary Animals, presented by Major Denham.
The Malayan Bear,
from Bencoolen: presented by Sir Thomas Stamford Raffles.—The only one in England.
Pair of Oriental Leopards,
Remarkable for their docility.

A beautiful Panther,
Presented by the Marchioness of Londonderry: the most exquisite Animal of the kind ever seen in Europe.
An enormous grisly Bear,
from Hudson's Bay, whose bulk exceeds that of an Ox.
Pair of Cinnamon Bears.
Pair of White Bears,
from the North Pole, commonly called the Sea Lion.
A fine black Bear,
from North America.

FOURTH DIVISION.

Contains a great variety of the Simia Tribe. A pair of large dog-faced Baboons. A large pig-tailed Baboon, ring-tailed Monkeys, Woolly Lemn, from Madagascar, Negro Monkeys, Kellitrix Monkeys, Chinese Bonnet Monkeys, a pair of Marmazette Monkeys; a pair of Coati Mondis, Ichneumon, Java Hares, Racoons, two Jackalls, or Lion Providers, from Africa, &c.

The Beast are regularly Fed at 3 in the Afternoon,
Which will be found the most interesting time.—NO EXTRA CHARGE.

N.B. The highest Prices given for every kind of Foreign Beast & Birds.
J. KING, Printer, College Hill, Upper Thames Street.

TRIFLES
FOR CHILDREN.

PART III.

News from the Tower!

SINCE we published the Second Part of Trifles for Children, one night a large leopard escaped from its den in the Tower of London, where it had been left by a gentleman. At first it attacked a
A

ABOVE LEFT 136. *Poster of 1826, advertising the Tower Menagerie, by then much enlarged after the appointment of Alfred Cops as Keeper in 1822. For the first time in the history of the Menagerie, animals were being purchased rather than arriving only as royal gifts.*

TOP RIGHT 137. *Engraving by Thomas Rowlandson of 1807 showing visitors arriving from Tower Hill at the Menagerie gate. A sign directing visitors to the 'Wild Beasts' can be seen on the right, and the Menagerie Keeper's house (right) and the Middle Tower (left) made out on the inside.*

MIDDLE RIGHT 138. *"Extraordinary and fatal combat" between a lion, a tiger and a tigress in December 1830, as illustrated in a contemporary lithograph. The caption relates that the "Lion was so seriously injured that he died in a few days afterwards".*

BOTTOM RIGHT 139. *Pages from a late eighteenth-century children's booklet reporting the escape of a leopard – apparently deposited at the Menagerie for safe keeping. The 'Spur Guard' (visible in the background with two chimneys) was a guardhouse, put up to the north of the Middle Tower in 1752.*

During the first twenty years of the nineteenth century the fortunes of the Menagerie declined, and by 1821 its inhabitants had diminished to four lions, a panther, a leopard, a grizzly bear and a tiger. The following year there was the beginning of a recovery with the appointment of Alfred Cops as Keeper, who, within a few years, amassed a collection embracing over 60 species and numbering more than 280 animals. But the recovery was short-lived, for in 1830 the decision was taken to close the Menagerie, and in 1831–32 those animals belonging to the Crown were presented to the newly established Zoological Society of London and transferred to their zoo, then being enlarged in Regent's Park. Cops continued to show his own collection for a few years, but under pressure from the Royal Household, the Keeper wrote to the Governor on 27 August 1835 confirming that "the Exhibition shall be closed tomorrow". The remaining animals were sold to an American showman and shipped across the Atlantic. After six hundred years the Tower Menagerie was no more.

The Wardrobe

One of the most spectacular sights that could be viewed at the Tower during the sixteenth century and up to the Civil War was the assemblage of royal clothes and furnishings administered by the Wardrobe. By the Tudor period, although the care of military equipment and the Jewel House had been apportioned to their own dedicated institutions – the Office of Ordnance and the Jewel House – the Great Wardrobe still retained an important repository, with its own staff, at the Tower. In 1617 the Master of the Great Wardrobe was described, in respect of the Tower, as having "custodie of all former Kings and Queenes auncient Robes remaining in the Tower of London, and all hangings of Arras, Tapestrie, or the like, for his Majesties houses, with bedding remaining in standing Wardrobes, as Hampton Court, Richmond &c".

In the Middle Ages the main repository may have been housed in the annexe attached to the east side of the White Tower, but in 1532, under Henry VIII, the Wardrobe's facilities were improved with the creation of a new storehouse stretching between the Broad Arrow and the Wardrobe towers (fig. 140). The inventory of Henry VIII's goods made on his death in 1547 shows the Tower Wardrobe to have contained numerous beds, carpets, cushions, chairs and canopies, and over 150 tapestries and wall-hangings. Many of these items were made with silver and gold cloth, velvet and damask, and some were even decorated with precious stones (fig. 142).

An array of such dazzling objects could not fail to attract attention, and visitors to the Tower were impressed by what they saw. In 1598 Paul Hentzner was shown "an immense quantity of bed-furniture, such as canopies; and the like, some of them most richly ornamented with pearl, some royal dresses so extremely magnificent, as to raise any one's admiration at the sums they must have cost". Two years later, among the items that impressed Baron Waldstein were "sixty tapestries very richly and splendidly worked with gold thread ... and numerous chairs which had their cushions woven in silk and gold thread".

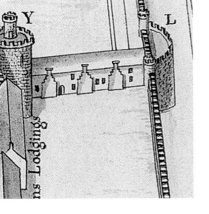

ABOVE 140. *Detail from the survey of 1597, showing the Wardrobe storehouse put up between the Wardrobe Tower (left, with turret) and the Broad Arrow Tower on the right.*

FAR RIGHT 141. *Elizabeth I in her coronation robes, which were kept at the Tower Wardrobe during her reign. Portrait by an unknown artist.*

RIGHT 142. *Entry in an inventory of the Tower Wardrobe's contents taken after Henry VIII's death in 1547 describing "a chair of timber covered with crimson cloth of gold tissue fringed with Venice gold having four pommels of silver and gilt, whereof two be crowned with Crowns Imperiall". Most of the treasures such as these were destroyed or dispersed in 1649 by the new republican regime.*

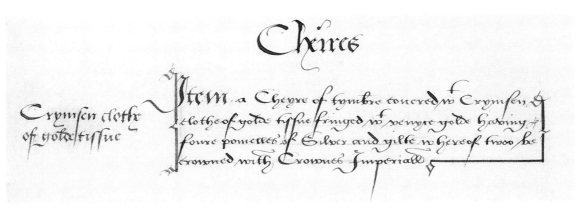

ABOVE LEFT 143. *A sixteenth-century French salt-cellar mentioned in a royal inventory of 1550, an example of the type of precious object stored at the Tower Jewel House until sold off or destroyed in 1649. The coronation regalia, newly re-created, came to be stored at the Tower only after the restoration of the monarchy in 1660.*

ABOVE RIGHT 144. *Detail of a portrait of Charles I by Daniel Mytens of 1631. The crown was probably the State Crown made for Henry VII or Henry VIII, kept at the Tower Jewel House until its destruction in 1649.*

OPPOSITE 145. *The Imperial State Crown, made for the coronation of George VI in 1937 and altered for Her Majesty Queen Elizabeth II in 1953.*

In 1649, following the execution of Charles I, the Council of State ordered the contents of the Tower Wardrobe, like those of the Jewel House, to be sold. The inventory made at the time shows just how valuable the contents were: they included hangings to the value of £18,000 (the price of several fully equipped warships) and £3000-worth of other textiles and miscellaneous furnishings. The Tower Wardrobe thus ceased to exist, and the following year the empty buildings were converted for the storage of gunpowder.

The Jewel House

One of the most famous of the Tower's attractions since the early sixteenth century has been an assemblage of the sovereign's jewels, plate and precious-metal objects used on ceremonial occasions. By the early sixteenth century the institution in charge of these, known as the Jewel House, had split off from the medieval Great Wardrobe (see above), and had established a permanent staff and storehouses at all the major palaces. Prior to the restoration of the monarchy in 1660, the most precious items, the coronation regalia, were kept at Westminster Abbey, but the state regalia – used on occasions other than the coronation – and a vast quantity of other jewels

and plate, were kept at the Tower. Although a repository had been provided by Henry VII in 1508, attached to south side of the White Tower, its accommodation at the Tower was largely rebuilt by Henry VIII in 1535. At this time iron bars were provided for the windows, chests for the department's records and scales for weighing precious metal and stones. These buildings – among them that identified as the 'Jewel House' on the plan of 1597 (fig. 55) – remained in use until the outbreak of the Civil War and survived until the Restoration, but their contents were soon to be destroyed or dispersed. In the summer of 1649 the jewels and plate at the Tower of London, and the regalia at Westminster, joined the contents of the Wardrobe among the king's goods to be disposed of by the new republican régime: the crowns were "totallie broken and defaced" and the metal was sent to the Mint to be made into coinage, while the other items were to be sold.

At the Restoration, all that could be recovered of the old regalia for the new King's coronation were the twelfth-century 'coronation spoon' and the ceremonial swords of Temporal Justice, Spiritual Justice and Mercy. The rest had to be entirely remade. The Jewel House premises, too, had to be repaired, and by September 1661 carpenters were "makeing ready of the Jewell house for the keeping of the Kings plate". In 1668, however, as a part of the initiative to clear the White Tower of attached buildings, the chimneys of which were seen as a danger to the powder stored inside it, the Master of the Jewel House was instructed to remove the regalia from the old building so that it could be demolished. The Master's complaint that there was no other place in the Tower to house the jewels obliged the Ordnance to convert the 'Irish Tower' – now the Martin Tower – into a new depository. The Crown Jewels were to be housed on the ground floor with the keeper's apartment above, and the existing second floor evidently dates from this time (fig. 160).

The practice of exhibiting the state regalia to members of the public, at least by special arrangement, no doubt originated in the Middle Ages and is certainly recorded in the early seventeenth century. It was only after the move to the Martin Tower, however, that arrangements were made for regular viewing. In the first years this was accompanied by a dangerous breakdown of security, and in the notori-

RIGHT 146. *The twelfth-century 'coronation spoon', the sole surviving item of regalia, apart from the ceremonial swords, to escape destruction in 1649. It was bought by a private individual at the sale of Charles I's goods in 1649 and returned to Charles II in 1660.*

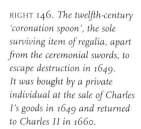

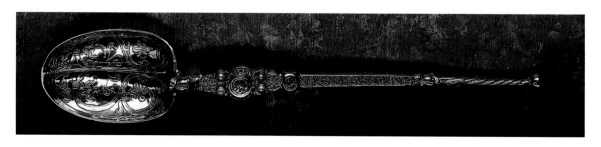

147. An engraving of c. 1820, showing the Crown Jewels as displayed in the Martin Tower from 1669 to 1842. The Yeoman Warder in the background is evidently extolling their splendours to the seated visitors. Note the State Crown and what appears to be the Exeter Salt displayed under glass domes on clockwork turntables.

ous incident of 1671 'Colonel' Thomas Blood, aided and abetted by a woman posing as his wife, almost succeeded in stealing the crown, orb and sceptre. Improvements to security evidently followed, and when Zacharias von Uffenbach visited the Tower in 1710 he described how, after entering "a gloomy and cramped den", a strong door was bolted from within, while sentries locked it from outside, and how visitors sat on wooden benches and viewed the jewels through "a trellis work of strong iron" (fig. 147).

148. A printed broadsheet from the reign of Queen Anne (1702–1714), advertising the splendours of the Jewel House.

A List of Her Majesties Regalia, besides Plate, and other Rich Things, at the Jewel-House in the Tower of London.

1 —— THE *Imperial Crown*, which all the Kings of *England* have been Crown'd with, ever since *Edward* the Confessor's Time.
2 —— The *Orb* or *Globe*, held in the Queens Left Hand at the Coronation; on the Top of which is a Jewel near an Inch and half in height.
3 —— The *Royal Scepter* with the *Cross*, which has another Jewel of great value under it.
4 —— The *Scepter* with the *Dove*, being the Emblem of Peace.
5 —— St. *Edward's Staff*, all beaten Gold, carried before the Queen at the Coronation.
6 —— A Rich *Salt-Seller of State*, the Figure of the *Tower*, used on the Queens Table at the Coronation.
7 —— *Curtana*, or the *Sword of Mercy*, born between the two Swords of Justice, the Spiritual, and Temporal, at the Coronation.
8 —— A Noble *Silver Font*, double Gilt, that the Queen and Royal Family were Christ'ned in.
9 —— A Large *Silver Fountain*, presented to King *Charles* the Second, by the Town of *Plymouth*.

10 —— THE Queens *Diadem*, or *Circlet*, which Her Majesty wore in proceeding to Her Coronation.
11 —— The *Coronation Crown*, made for the late Queen *Mary*.
12 —— The Rich *Crown of State* that Her Majesty wears on Her Throne in Parliament, in which is a large Emerald 7 Inches round, a Pearl, the finest in the World, and a Ruby of inestimable value.
13 —— A *Globe* and *Scepter* made for the late Queen *Mary*.
14 —— An *Ivory Scepter* with a *Dove*, made for the late King *James's* Queen.
15 —— The *Golden Spurs* and the *Armillas*, that are wore at the Coronation.
16 —— The *Ampulla*, or *Eagle of Gold*, which holds the Holy Oyl that the Kings and Queens are Anointed with, and the *Golden Spoon* that the Bishop pours the Oyl into. Which are great Pieces of Antiquity.

Some care had evidently been taken to display the jewels, Von Uffenbach also noting that the display "looks very well and sparkles charmingly because they have lights there on account of the gloom".

Not all visitors, however, were so impressed. William Hutton, for example, describes being taken in 1784 to "a door in an obscure corner" that led to "a dismal hole resembling the cell of the condemned", and the Jewel House and its presentation continued to attract criticism well into the nineteenth century. One of the most damning accounts was published in 1821 by Christian Goede in *A Foreigner's Opinion of England*. Goede describes going to "a dark gloomy place, and there left waiting in the most eager expectation". He goes on to contemplate the visitor's

astonishment when all of a sudden the ghastly figure of an old woman with a candle in her hand appears before him. He may perhaps imagine for a moment that there is some farce going forward; and that the witch of Endor will instantaneously conjure up a heap of hidden treasures to his ravished sight. But he is quickly undeceived ... the woman takes some sceptres and crowns out of a couple of old boxes, shows them to him through an iron grate, and chants with a shrill voice the list and story of these wonderful curiosities, with which the whole farce is most stupidly concluded.

The lady custodian may have been the "old hag" described by an American visitor in 1830 as someone who "presided like a high priestess over their glories". The same visitor went on to mock her mechanical performance: "She began in a most solemn, measured tone – 'Ladies and Gentlemen, please to attend the explanation' – but the ladies were somewhat overcome by the pompous manner ... and laughed outright." Another visitor "would ask her a great many questions as she went on", which forced her "to go back again and start anew, again and again, to the great amusement of her tormentor".

In 1840, not before time, the Lord Chamberlain's Office determined that a more commodious and secure home was needed for the regalia. Under an unusual arrangement, the Royal Engineers designed and directed the construction of a new Jewel House, their costs being met with surplus fees from public admission charges. The new Gothic-style building was attached to the south side of the Martin Tower, with its elaborate crenellated entrance and flanking towers within the Inner Ward, but with the actual strongroom standing on a brick vault within the Outer Ward (figs. 149 and 150). The rooms for the

Jewel Keeper and his family were over the Jewel Chamber and linked to the Martin Tower. The new building, opened to the public early in 1842, proved, however, to be anything but a success. It was plagued with defects, including damp and poor lighting, while inspections revealed that the building was not properly fireproofed or even secure against theft. Less than ten years later the Duke of Wellington proposed its demolition, but another decade was to pass before a better arrangement could be provided.

By September 1866 it had been decided to move the regalia to the Wakefield Tower, after plans prepared by the architect Anthony Salvin for a new Jewel House on the site of the 1840–41 building had been rejected. Work began in 1867: the operation involved replacing the original timber first floor with a reinforced brick vault to support the jewel display, the introduction of the existing ceiling vault to the first-floor chamber, the construction of a covered entrance (now demol-

BELOW 149. *The ill-fated Jewel House of 1841, found to be completely unsatisfactory and pulled down in 1870.*

BOTTOM 150. *The Crown Jewels as displayed in the Jewel House of 1841.*

ABOVE 151. *Photograph of c. 1905 showing the Crown Jewels as displayed in the upper chamber of the Wakefield Tower after 1870.*

ished) against the north side of the tower, and the provision of the surviving stone bridge to link the Jewel Chamber with the upper floor of St Thomas's Tower – the latter being converted into a residence for the Jewel Keeper. Messrs Brown & Downing, iron-founders of Birmingham, provided the great cage, railings, gate and barriers behind which the regalia were put on display in January 1870 (fig. 151).

The cage was retained until 1910–11, when it was replaced by a reinforced glass case for greater security and easier viewing. By the 1960s, however, the volume of visitors was such that new accommodation was clearly needed, and in 1967 a new purpose-built Jewel House was opened underneath the Waterloo Barracks, in which the exhibits could be displayed to far greater effect. This was in turn replaced by the existing arrangement, within the same building, in 1994.

Myth and misconception

A mighty fortress filled with fearsome weaponry, the residence of kings, a place of safety for their jewels, and – from time to time – their prisoners, the Tower of London was held in awe by the public from the earliest years. In the Middle Ages this is reflected by the attribution of the Tower not to William the Conqueror, but to Julius Caesar, or – more exotic still – refugees from the fall of Troy. The same awesome reputation must, for example, have prompted the Londoners' fantastical idea, related by Matthew Paris, that the new defensive works of 1240 (see pp. 27–29) contained "many cells ... for the imprisonment of large numbers separately, so that none of them could speak to each other" and in which recalcitrant citizens would be thrown into chains.

In the sixteenth century it was spelled out by the London historian John Stow that the White Tower, at least, dated from the time of the Conqueror, and for the next two centuries there was relatively little deliberate cultivation of myth and legend, although growing public interest in Henry VIII, in particular, attracted increasing numbers to see his armours and other memorabilia. Early guidebooks and accounts of the Tower dating from the eighteenth century are peppered with anecdote, but on the whole these are set down in a brief and unemotional manner. Towards the end of the century, however, a change can be detected, partly as a result of a growing interest in British history and in the Middle Ages and Tudor period particularly. In 1786, for example, the painter James Northcote produced a scene of the *Little Princes in the Tower*, the first of several commissions in a melodramatic Gothic style, foreshadowing the profusion of pictures and engravings of the nineteenth century. When, in 1825, John Bayley published the *History and Antiquities of the Tower of London* – the first serious monograph on the castle – he still felt it necessary to devote half the work to an account of imprisonment, torture and execution. Further publications in the same vein were to follow, but the popular misconception of the Tower – and thus the deliberate process of myth-making – really took off after the publication in 1840 of Harrison Ainsworth's *The Tower of London: A Historical Romance*. Based on the story of the accession, deposition and execution of Lady Jane Grey, the Tower was first and foremost the

RIGHT 152. *The murder of the 'Princes in the Tower', Edward V and his brother Richard, as imagined by the painter James Northcote in about 1790.*

FAR RIGHT 153. *Late nineteenth-century painting by Emily Mary Osborn showing the Jacobite Lord Nithsdale's escape from the Tower in 1716. Although in this case representing a true story, images of this sort responded to and perpetuated a romanticized view of the castle's past and its role as a place of imprisonment.*

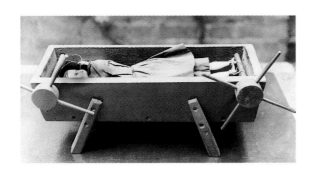

RIGHT 154. *A miniature rack made for public display in the second half of the nineteenth century, in response to the ever-increasing public interest in the darker side of the Tower's history. The real item – disused since 1640 – had by then been long destroyed.*

setting for an endless series of heart-rending events and foul play. The author tells of dungeons (though in fact the Tower has very few basement rooms) and of a time when "Tower Hill boasted a scaffold, and its soil was dyed with the richest and best blood in the land". Such fantasies, backed by the relentless march of the romantic movement, helped create and fuel an ever-increasing demand to see and experience the scene of such events. When, even in the case of a real event that actually took place at the Tower, neither the premises nor material any longer existed, it had to be invented. The Queen's House, for example, the only remaining sixteenth-century building in the castle, became associated with every one of the Tower's famous prisoners: among its attractions was Anne Boleyn's bedroom, although in fact it was built four years after her execution, while the Council Chamber was identified as the scene of Guy Fawkes's interrogation in 1605, although the room in question was not created until the insertion of the existing second floor in 1607.

By the early twentieth century it was being explained that Thomas More, although certainly a Tower prisoner, had been confined in the lower chamber of the Bell Tower, although the evidence for this is at least open to question; by the mid-nineteenth century it was held that Princess Elizabeth had been held in the tower's upper chamber from Palm Sunday until 19 May 1554, when in fact she was almost certainly lodged in part of the royal lodgings that survived at the other end of the castle. The Tower and the public authorities also responded enthusiastically to the new popular demand. The notional scaffold site on Tower Green was railed off and marked with a plaque in 1866 (fig. 155), while a plethora of signs appeared attributing certain rooms and spaces to various events. The desire to meet visitor expectations of this sort extended to the displays as well: in the middle of the nineteenth century, various instruments of torture and a notorious fake known as the 'Executioner's mask' were added to the display in the Spanish Armoury, while miniature racks were made in default of any original (fig. 154).

Today, although more accurate and no less interesting information is provided, the visitor may still enjoy the sense of drama and the atmosphere that has encouraged and been enhanced by centuries of enthusiastic myth-making and embellishment.

MIDDLE 155. *A Yeoman Warder shows the scaffold site to a group of visitors in 1895. Although a fitting reminder of the executions that took place within the Tower, no permanent scaffold in fact existed, and no more than seven such events within the castle precincts are actually recorded.*

BOTTOM 156. *A Yeoman Warder explains the bloody history of the execution block to a group of children in the 1860s, evidently captivating the three small boys on the left (although the little girl on the right seems less enthusiastic). Generations of children have been imbued with the sinister side of the*
Tower's history, perpetuating the myth that it was almost exclusively a place of dark deeds, torture and execution. Painting by George Bernard O'Neil (1828–1917).

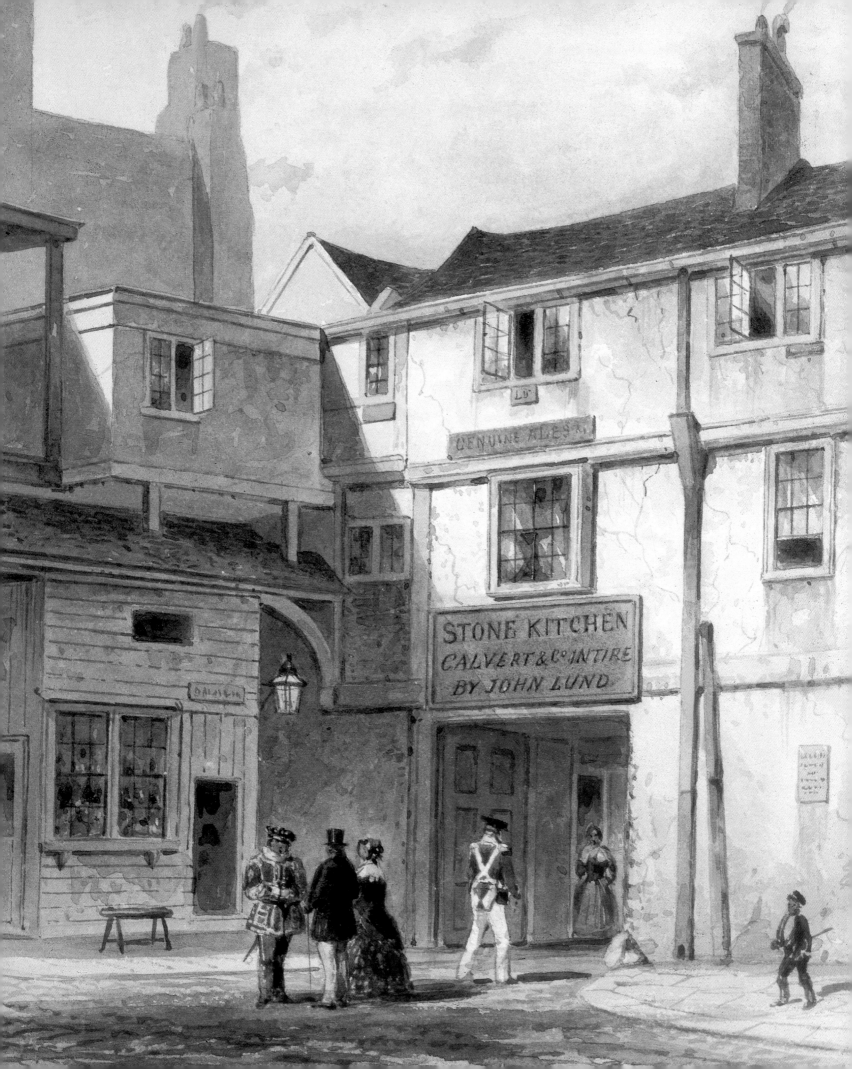

The Tower
COMMUNITY

The variety and importance of the Tower's many roles are mirrored by the diversity of its residents and workforce: officials, soldiers, Yeoman Warders, artisans and servants.

LEFT 157. *View of the Stone Kitchen, a tavern housed in a building at the south end of Mint Street, between the Byward and the Bell towers. From at least the late seventeenth century the Stone Kitchen, along with the Golden Chain (both closed 1846), served many generations of the Tower's community. Watercolour by Thomas Hosmer Shepherd (1792–1864).*

RIGHT 158. *View across Tower Green of 1720, showing the large house built in 1540 for the Lieutenant and now occupied by the Resident Governor. Currently known as the Queen's House, the name changes according to whether the sovereign is king or queen.*

Since the very beginning there have been both permanent and occasional residents at the Tower, including at least the Constable, his staff, and very probably a chaplain. By the end of the thirteenth century it is likely that many of the staff of the Mint, the Wardrobe and the Ordnance also lived within the walls, and from at least the late fifteenth century residence may have been required of the Yeoman Warders. At all times, of course, the Tower's community has been swelled by those who work but do not actually live there.

The most important resident during much of the castle's history was the Constable, since 1784 a senior officer in the army and frequently a peer of the realm. The earliest twelfth-century incumbents may have lodged in the White Tower (see p. 18), but by the late twelfth century the Constable had a house in the bailey, rebuilt in the 1360s. To what extent the medieval Constables were expected to be resident is unclear, but instructions issued in 1555 set down that he was then "to be contynually Resident upon his offyce wthin the sayde tower of London" and "to have the charge and governance of the saide Tower and of their ma[jes]^{ties} Lodgings and all the prisoners there". By this date, however, it was the Constable's deputy, the Lieutenant, who was effectively responsible for the day-to-day running of the Tower, and at the start of Elizabeth I's reign the office of Constable was allowed to lapse, being revived only in 1682. The residence of the Lieutenant, the present Queen's House (fig. 159)

– built in 1540 on the site of the fourteenth-century Constable's lodgings – is an important survival from the Tudor period (and incidentally the most important example of timber-framed domestic architecture to have survived the Great Fire of 1666). Reporting to the Lieutenant was the Deputy Lieutenant and the Major of the Garrison, the former being the more senior, and who, by the second half of the eighteenth century had been elevated to the status of Resident Governor and was living in the Queen's House. In the nineteenth century, however, after a period of divided authority, the situation was reversed, the post of Major being combined with that of Resident Governor (1858) and the Deputy Lieutenantship abolished.

LEFT When Viscount Dillon was appointed the first Curator of the Armouries in 1892 he proceeded to try on many of the suits of armour himself.

RIGHT Sir John Fox Burgoyne, Constable of the Tower (1865–71), has the unique distinction of a memorial in the Chapel of St Peter ad Vincula, alongside three queens.

The Mace carried by the Chief Yeoman Warder was purchased by the inhabitants of the Tower Liberties in 1792.

159. *View across Tower Green from the north. The Queen's House, with its external rendering removed and its timber framing revealed, is shown straight ahead; to the left are the two warders' houses put up by Salvin in the 1860s.*

160. *Interior of the Jewel House Keeper's lodging on the top floor of the Martin Tower in about 1840 – a picture of early Victorian comfort, and typical of the way in which the Tower's medieval interiors had been adapted by that time.*

Below the senior officers there were large number of other individuals with official duties. An important example was the Porter: as his title suggests (derived from the French *porte* or *portier*), he was responsible for the security of the gates and for disarming visitors coming into the fortress. As such, he was lodged by the main western entrance, being provided in the 1480s with a house in the new Bulwark (see p. 46), and after its demolition with space in the western entrance buildings. The last official Porter's residence can be seen on a drawing of 1845, attached to the south side of the Middle Tower (fig. 161). But the best-known members of the Tower's official community are the Yeoman Warders, popularly known since at least 1700 as 'Beefeaters'. Originally forming part of the royal bodyguard (see p. 47), with the Tower's decline as a royal residence their duties came to be more concerned with warding the gates and state prisoners. The connection with the royal household has not, however, been completely severed, and to this day the Yeoman Warders undertake periodic, extraordinary duties alongside the Yeomen of the Guard. The Constable's instructions for 1555 required there to be twenty-one "discreet, trusty and personable yeomen of middle age", none "above fifty or below thirty". Seven were to be appointed Chief Yeoman Warders and provided with lodgings, the rest to have chambers only. They were to receive 8d daily and a livery coat the same as the ordinary Yeomen of the Guard and "other profits of their majesties reward over and above the wages aforesaid". The Chief Yeoman Warders received an additional 40s per annum. These provi-

sions seem to have altered little by the end of the sixteenth century, and in 1598 Sir John Peyton, the Lieutenant of the Tower, complained that at a time "wherein the price of all things and all mens labors are increased they [the Warders] are growne to exceeding povertie". He did, however, go on to complain that among the Warders were "divers unfitt for the place; some of them utterly neglectinge their duties in service others given to drunckeness, disorders and quarrells". Some were said to be physically unfit, or involved with other employments, which resulted in the warding of the Tower being much weakened. Further efforts to improve matters followed in succeeding centuries, but fundamental reform of the payment and appointment system, and the enforcement of the conditions of residence had to await the arrival of the Duke of Wellington in 1826. The process whereby the post of Yeoman Warder was handed down through the family or sold was abolished, with the order that, in future, the post was to be occupied by worthy non-commissioned officers of the Household Cavalry, Foot Guards and Infantry of the Line, solely of their regiment's recommendations. Ten years later the Master-General of the Ordnance began the process of removing certain privileges when he awarded the Warders £722 10s for conducting visitors to the armouries "in lieu of all payments received hitherto from visitors to the Tower".

The spiritual needs of the Tower community were provided for by the Chapel of St Peter ad Vincula – the "Parish church within the Tower of London", as it was defined under Henry VIII – as it still does today. The chapel was served by a chaplain, now lodged in a house built in 1749 to replace a timber parsonage of 1616–17 on the same site.

In addition to its official and semi-official residents, the Tower also accommodated many of the craftsmen working, in particular, for the Mint and the Ordnance – in addition to their dependants. A glimpse of this vast army is given by the list of tradesmen required for sentry duty in the *Orders for the*

LEFT 161. *Elevation of the western entrance to the Tower in 1845 showing the Spur Guard to the left of the Middle Tower and the Porter's lodge to the right.*

163. *Yeoman Warders in state dress, holding their traditional weapon, the partisan.*

162. *The Ceremony of the Keys in 1898, showing the Chief Yeoman Warder and his escort during the final stages of the ceremony.*

Government of the Tower of 1555, which includes – in addition to the castle's gunners – surveyors' clerks, wardrobe keepers, bowyers, fletchers, gunpowder makers, smiths, joiners, pike makers, spear makers and wheelwrights – the officers of the Mint making a money payment instead. The chapel register also offers many fascinating insights into the inhabitants of the Tower, some famous, but most very ordinary, who have been baptised, married and buried at the chapel over the centuries. But no single document better illustrates the character and diversity of the once-thriving community than the survey of the Tower conducted for the first national census in June 1841. This reveals that on the night of 6 June there were some 556 souls asleep in the barracks, including 77 women and children. Five days later the civilian presence in the fortress numbered 474 people living in 75 properties. Of these, 189 were males and 283 females. Their ages ranged from William Lee, aged 14 days, to Ann Lannan, aged 78. In addition to the Resident Governor, the Chaplain, the Yeoman Warders, and the Master Gunner, the survey lists the occupations of the male residents as clerks and messengers, salesmen, tailors, shopkeepers, innkeepers, bricklayers, labourers, a carpenter, a painter, a plasterer, a smith, an engineer, a barrack master, a barrister, a tool inspector, a warehouseman, a draper, a cigar maker, a tobacco maker, a brush maker, a lamplighter, a gun maker and a ticket office keeper. Most of the working women are listed as domestic servants, housekeepers and charwomen, though there is a governess, a nurse, a flower maker and, last, a 75-year-old silk hand-loom weaver named Ann Hurd.

The Castle
RESTORED

In the wake of the growing interest in the Middle Ages,
the accretions of centuries are swept away after 1845, and
the Tower's thirteenth-century splendours are revealed or
re-created.

LEFT 164. *View of the Beauchamp Tower in 1898, with all later accretions cleared away and the windows, battlements and other features restored to what Salvin considered to be their original appearance.*

RIGHT 165. *View of the Beauchamp Tower from the Inner Ward shortly before Salvin's work of 1852. By this time only the pointed hood-moulding over the central window betrayed its thirteenth-century origins.*

There had been a growing interest in England's medieval past in the eighteenth century, and an increasing, although generally fanciful, borrowing from Gothic architecture. By the middle of the next century, however, thanks to the popular enthusiasm for the Middle Ages fostered by such authors as Sir Walter Scott, and the now-meticulous study of its form and detail, neo-Gothic architecture became both fashionable and accurate. It was this movement, coinciding with a new scholarly interest in the Tower's history and the withdrawal of many of the institutions that had overcrowded it for centuries, that led, between about 1845 and 1885, to its greatest transformation since the thirteenth century: most of the houses, offices and warehouses that concealed its ancient fabric were demolished, and large parts of the castle given, for better or for worse, the pristine "medieval" appearance they retain today.

The process began in the first decades of the nineteenth century with the piecemeal appearance of new work in a Gothic style, beginning with the New Horse Armoury, put up against the south side of the White Tower in 1825 (fig. 66). The Main Guard, built alongside the west face of the same building in 1717, together with the old storehouse of 1670–71 immediately to the south (see p. 62), were subsequently remodelled to match the Horse Armoury, and in 1840 work began on the short-lived new Jewel House by the Martin Tower (fig. 149). The style of the Waterloo Barracks and the adjacent officers' block,

Beauchamp Tower from the East

built between 1845 and 1850 (see p. 80), the former in what a contemporary described as "castellated Gothic of the 15th century", also reflected the new fashion.

In the second half of the century still greater opportunities for reconstruction were provided by the gradual phasing out of the manufacturing activities and storage facilities of the Ordnance Office (taken over by the War Office in 1855) and the with-

LEFT Prince Albert thought it was inappropriate to use the Tower for the storage of munitions and "desired to have it preserved purely as an ancient monument".

RIGHT Salvin was awarded the Royal Gold Medal of the Institute of British Architects in 1863 for his work at the Tower.

In 1868 the authorities delayed the restoration of the Chapel of St Peter ad Vincula because of the "extraordinary demands for the Abyssinian Expedition".

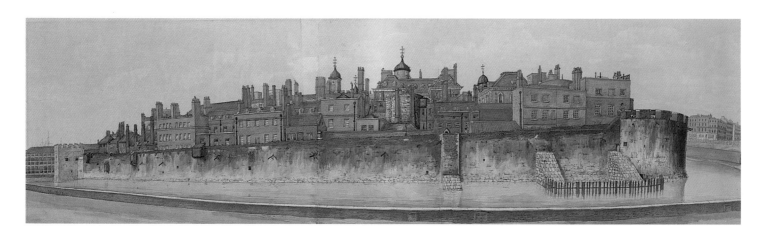

166. *View of the Tower from the east in 1826, showing the extent to which the castle's medieval fabric had disappeared under a mass of later accretions. Watercolour by J. Tugman.*

drawal, in particular, of the Record Office by 1858 (see p. 89). The renewed process began with the Office of Works' appointment of the architect Anthony Salvin, already an established exponent of the Later Gothic Revival. His first commission was awarded in response to the author Harrison Ainsworth's suggestion to the Tower authorities that the gigantic Beauchamp Tower, on the western inner curtain wall, should be made suitable for the public display of the sixteenth- and seventeenth-century prisoners' inscriptions inside: Salvin studied the building in April 1851, and in the following year had two warders' houses against the east face pulled down, the exterior walls refaced, its windows and doorways replaced, and the battlements re-created (figs. 164 and 165).

The next phase of work was brought about by a visit to the Tower by Queen Victoria's husband, Prince Albert, to view the condition of the thirteenth-

167. *The Salt Tower in 1846, during the demolition of various buildings put up against it and a stretch of Henry III's curtain wall.*

century Salt Tower, by now in a state of near collapse. Keenly interested in architecture, the Prince's opinion was that it should be restored, but that the work should be seen as part of a comprehensive restoration of the medieval defences under the control of a single architect: Salvin was selected, and work to the Salt Tower was completed in 1858 (fig. 167). Meanwhile, further work had been planned or undertaken, in the spirit of Prince Albert's suggestion, beginning with the replacement of the buildings lining the outer curtain wall between the North Bastion and Brass Mount to Salvin's designs in 1857. In 1858 Salvin's attention was turned to the White Tower (fig. 168), where the top floor, now vacated by the Record Office, was cleared of props and the main roof beams reinforced by iron girders, their ends supported by decorative brackets (since removed). The Chapel of St John the Evangelist was taken in hand in 1864, when Salvin had the internal walls scoured of all accretions and repaired, and the windows embellished in a twelfth-century style (fig. 16). Elsewhere in the castle, in June 1862 St Thomas's Tower required immediate remedial works after the partial collapse of the south-east turret, leading to a major restoration of the building between 1864 and 1866: much of the exterior was refaced, the battlements and turrets reset and new, medieval-style, windows introduced, giving the building the appearance it retains to this day (fig. 40). Towards the end of 1866 various old buildings to the west of the Bloody Tower were pulled down, and on part of the site Salvin erected new warders' houses – the present nos. 7 and 8 Tower Green (fig. 159). At the same time he was supervising various alterations along the riverside wall, including the introduction of medieval-style crenellations and the re-forming of the East Drawbridge. The last major work of the then elderly architect was the restoration of the Wakefield Tower between 1867 and 1869.

Salvin's immediate successor was the Office of Works architect John Taylor. Although later knighted for his work on public buildings, Taylor's ruthless approach to 'restoration' led to the destruction of

168. Scheme of 1857 by
Anthony Salvin for restoring
the north elevation of the
White Tower. In the event, the
'Norman'-style surrounds of
the type shown were only used

on the chapel windows –
fortunately, as the original ones
were quite different and their
seventeenth- and eighteenth-
century replacements of interest
in their own right.

RIGHT 169. *Photograph showing the interior of the Chapel of St Peter ad Vincula before the alterations of 1876–77, then still complete with its seventeenth-century reredos and eighteenth-century pews and gallery.*

BELOW 170. *Photograph of the chapel interior from a similar viewpoint, showing the results of John Taylor's work.*

important buildings at the Tower simply because they failed to live up to his own ideals of medieval architecture. One of his first projects, in 1876–77, concerned the long-awaited restoration of the Chapel of St Peter ad Vincula, which had by then become seriously dilapidated. Taylor's solution, however, went far beyond structural repair, and included the removal of the eighteenth-century gallery and box pews, and the Baroque pulpit, reading desk and pedimented reredos (figs. 169 and 170).

In 1878 Taylor resumed Salvin's work on the riverside curtain wall. An upper floor was reinstated on the Cradle Tower, and the river entrance on the floor below unblocked; the walls of the upper floor of the Well Tower were largely dismantled, rebuilt and capped with a concrete roof, while the curtain walls either side were repaired and their seventeenth-century gun ports replaced with imitation battlements. Lastly, the East Drawbridge gateway was again remodelled (to its present form) and the wharf, cleared of its remaining buildings, planted with planes and laid out as a public esplanade. A year later Taylor authorized the pulling down of the large stone building annexed to the east side of the White Tower – very probably of fourteenth-century origin – and with it much of the twelfth-century Wardrobe Tower that had survived embedded in its south-east angle.

Following the demolition of the vast eighteenth-century Ordnance Office that stood in the area to the south of the White Tower in the former Inmost Ward, work began on Taylor's most contentious project of all: the 'reconstruction' of the inner curtain wall between the Salt and Wakefield towers. Taylor's scheme involved the demolition of the building attached to the east side of the Wakefield Tower, formerly the Record House, and its replacement with a new curtain wall further to the north on a different alignment. What he failed to understand, or probably chose to ignore, was that the front face of the Record House was in fact no less than the thirteenth-century curtain wall, and that the rooms behind and above it were an important remnant of the medieval palace. But in spite of a celebrated dispute with the newly-established Society for the Protection of Ancient Buildings (SPAB), which attempted to point out the folly of the scheme to the architect and his client, the Office of Works, Taylor had his way: the Record House and the adjoining storehouse were demolished and the construction of the curtain wall to the west of the Lanthorn Tower began in 1885 and was completed in 1888 (fig. 172). The reconstructed defences, with their 'crazy paving' facing and wall walks carried on fanciful arcades, provide an excellent view of the river and the White Tower, but are a poor substitute for the real buildings they replace. This was to be the last phase of the 're-medievalization' process, however, for by the 1890s the prediction of the SPAB's secretary in 1883 "that the notion of building a medieval Tower to show what England was like in the 13th century will finally be given up and in place of it a respect for genuine remains of former times will prevail" was soon to be fulfilled.

The Tower in the
TWENTIETH CENTURY

Public recognition of the Tower's status as a national symbol and ancient monument stimulates a vast increase in visitors, demanding and encouraging changes in the way it is displayed and managed.

LEFT 173. *The Ceremony of the Keys (see fig. 162), shown at the point immediately before the ceremonial locking of the Byward Tower gates by the Chief Yeoman Warder, escorted in this instance by the Sergeant of the Guard, Sergeant White, and soldiers of the Nijmegen Company, Grenadier Guards.*

BELOW 174. *One of several artist's impressions prepared in 1913 for a teahouse at the western entrance – a project that was halted by the outbreak of the First World War.*

The last hundred years have seen the consolidation of the Tower's role as an ancient monument and visitor attraction rather than as a working fortress. At the same time conservation, rather than restoration and rebuilding, has resulted in fewer and fewer obtrusive and unnecessary alterations to its fabric, while the way in which the buildings and their contents are presented have changed so that the visitor can better understand what he or she sees.

Old habits die hard, however, and in the years either side of the First World War some rather heavy-handed works were undertaken, including the removal of the impressive 1850s clock faces from the north-east turret of the White Tower in 1913 (fig. 66), followed by alterations to the Queen's House and the stripping of the Byward Tower of interesting accretions in the 1920s. An ambitious scheme to rearrange the approaches to the western entrance (fig. 174) was halted by the First World War (1914–18), although partially resumed afterwards with excavations to the north of the Byward Tower, revealing the medieval causeway and remnants of the Lion Tower. Whereas the only German bomb to fall on the Tower during the First World War landed harmlessly in the moat, the aerial bombardment of the Second World War (1939–45) caused considerable damage: on 23 September 1940 high-explosive bombs destroyed the former eighteenth-century office of the Master Assayer of the Mint in the western Outer Ward, and the northern part of the Old Hospital Block to the east of the White Tower, while on 1 October the southern extent of the 1834 tramway was destroyed by a bomb, narrowly missing the White Tower. Two days later the massive North Bastion was blown apart (fig. 176), followed in December by the burning of the Main Guard, victim of an air raid during which over fifty incendiary devices fell within the fortress. Although the Tower's role as a place of imprisonment and execution had staged something of a revival during the First World War, it ended in 1941 with the confinement in the Queen's House of Rudolf Hess, Hitler's Deputy Reichsführer, for four days in May, and the death of the spy Joseph Jakobs on 14 August, shot in the Miniature Rifle Range that stood in the Outer Ward between the Constable and Martin towers.

LEFT In August 1939 the Crown Jewels and the most valuable objects in the Armouries were moved out of the Tower to a secret location.

RIGHT During the Second World War the basement of the White Tower was used as an air-raid shelter and provided sleeping accommodation for military personnel.

In 1994 the new £10 million Jewel House was opened at the Tower by Her Majesty The Queen.

After the War, and with the debris cleared and damage made good, the Tower of London reopened its gates and resumed life as one of the nation's favourite tourist attractions. But the steady growth in tourism has been achieved, to some extent, at the expense of what remained of the institutional life of the fortress: one of the Tower's oldest roles, as a military supply base, came to an end in 1994 with the withdrawal of the Royal Logistic Corps, and the last of the official skilled craftsmen closed their workshops and departed in 1984, while the garrison, although for other reasons, has dwindled to a small contingent retained for guard and ceremonial duties. Twelve years later, most of the Tower Armouries staff (renamed Royal Armouries in 1985) and much of the collection of arms and armour departed for a purpose-built museum in Leeds in Yorkshire.

The Tower still remains a living institution, however, managed by the Resident Governor and his staff, inhabited by over one hundred people – with at least two hundred working there during the day – and with a rich ceremonial life that continues unabated (figs. 178 and 179). It remains, too, the headquarters of the Royal Regiment of Fusiliers, raised there in 1685, while the Royal Armouries continues to display an important part of its collection in the White Tower. In addition, its changing role has provided opportunities to open new parts of the castle to public view, to improve the display of its treasures, to investigate its past, and in doing so to enhance visitors' understanding of the unique and fascinating history of the Tower of London.

ABOVE 175. *The east side of the Byward Tower in about 1890, then still complete with the balconies and other picturesque accretions swept away in the 1920s.*

RIGHT 176. *The mid-nineteenth-century North Bastion after being struck by a German bomb in October 1940.*

LEFT 177. *Tower Bridge viewed from the south-west. Built following an Act of Parliament in 1885, it has overshadowed the Tower since 1894, anticipating more radical and perhaps less welcome changes to the castle's surroundings in the twentieth century. Described in the year of its opening, as "a discredit to the generation which built it", it is now as well known as the castle itself.*

BELOW 178. *The Installation of the Field Marshal the Lord Inge of Richmond as Constable of the Tower of London in October 1996, at the point where the Lord Chamberlain (standing to the right) presents him with the ceremonial gold keys of the castle.*

RIGHT 179. *A gun salute on Tower wharf in the 1990s, continuing a tradition established at least as early as the 1530s. Salutes are fired on royal anniversaries (62 rounds), on the State opening of Parliament and to mark visits by foreign heads of state (41 rounds).*

GLOSSARY

bailey: a walled enclosure or courtyard of a castle.

barbican: an outer defence protecting the entrance to a castle.

bastion: a projecting part of a fortress, especially one at the angle of a wall, from which the ground before the wall or rampart is defended.

curtain wall: a wall enclosing a castle or one of its parts.

dendrochronology: the science of dating timber by comparing the width of its annual growth rings (different every year) to a known and dated sequence.

embrasure: a recess for a window, door *etc.*, or a small opening in a defensive wall or parapet (usually splayed on the inside) used as a shooting position.

keep: a relatively large tower within a castle, usually intended as a residence and its innermost stronghold. A typical feature of military architecture in the eleventh, twelfth and thirteenth centuries.

mural gallery: a gallery constructed within the thickness of a wall.

palisade: a strong fence made of stakes driven into the ground, especially for defence.

parapet: a low wall or railing along the edge of a roof, balcony *etc.*

rampart: a protective stone, earth or timber wall surrounding a fortress.

revetment: a retaining wall built to support or hold back a mass of earth or water.

FURTHER READING

In print:

Beaumont James, T., *The Palaces of Medieval England*, Seaby, 1990

Blair, C. (ed), *The Crown Jewels*, HMSO, 1998

Parnell, G., *The Tower of London, Past & Present*, Sutton Publishing, 1998

Parnell, G., *The Royal Menagerie at the Tower of London*, Royal Armouries, 1999

Thompson, M.W., *The Rise of the Castle*, Cambridge University Press, 1991

Thurley, S., *The Royal Palaces of Tudor England*, Yale University Press, 1993

Available in libraries:

Allen Brown, R., *The Castle in England*, 3rd edn, London, 1976

Bayley, J., *The History and Antiquities of the Tower of London*, 2 vols, 1829

Charlton, J. (ed), *The Tower of London: Its Buildings and Institutions*, HMSO, 1977

Colvin, H. (ed), *The History of the King's Works*, vols. I–V, HMSO, 1963–76

Parnell, G., *The Tower of London*, Batsford, 1993

Rouse, A.L., *The Tower of London in the History of the Nation*, Weidenfeld and Nicolson, 1972

INDEX

ACKNOWLEDGEMENTS

The authors and publishers would like to thank all those members of the Royal Armouries and Historic Royal Palaces staff and others who have contributed in any way to the preparation of this book and its content. Particular thanks go to Anna Keay who has shared the results of personal and unpublished research with particular generosity; and to Jeremy Ashbee, Jenny Band, Geoffrey Field, Christopher Gidlow, Aidan Lawes and Derek Renn for much information and comment. Many thanks are also due to Annie Heron for assistance with obtaining illustrations, to Cliff Birtchnell, Jonathan Buckmaster and David Ward for photography and to Clare Murphy for managing the picture research and editing the text.

HALF-TITLE: *The former gateway to the river beneath St Thomas's Tower, known by 1663 as 'Traitors' Gate'. Popularly associated with the arrival at the Tower of doomed and romantic figures such as Thomas More or Lady Jane Grey, this had in fact ceased to be the main access from the river by the mid-fourteenth century.*

FRONTISPIECE: *detail, fig. 130*

PAGE 6: *detail, fig. 79*

PAGES 8–9: *detail, fig. 18*

First published in 2000 by
Merrell Publishers Limited
42 Southwark Street
London SE1 1UN

in association with

Historic Royal Palaces
Hampton Court Palace
Surrey KT8 9AU

Distributed in the USA and Canada by Rizzoli International Publications, Inc.
through St Martin's Press, 175 Fifth Avenue, New York, New York 10010

British Library Cataloguing-in-Publication data
Impey, Edward
The Tower of London : the official illustrated history
1.Tower of London
I.Title II.Parnell, Geoffrey III.Historic Royal Palaces
942.1'2
ISBN 1 85894 106 7

Edited by Clare Murphy and Julian Honer
Designed by Maggi Smith and Stephen Coates

Produced by Merrell Publishers Limited

Printed and bound in Italy

PICTURE CREDITS

Aerofilms Limited: fig. 20; © The Board of Trustees of the Armouries: figs. 63, 71, 73, 74 (Frank Gardiner), 77, 78, 82 (XII.3090), 91, 92, 97, 119, 124, 125 (I.45), 126, 129 (XIX.17), 133, 135, 136, 151, 158, 160; Ashmolean Museum, Oxford: fig. 58; Bayerische Staatsgemäldesammlungen. Photograph by Blauel/Gnamm-Artothek: fig. 60; Renaud Beffeyte: fig. 22; Cliché Bibliothèque nationale de France: fig. 46; Birmingham Library Services: figs. 99, 101, 154, 164; Bodleian Library, University of Oxford (Gough Maps 21, fol. 40v (lower drawing)): fig. 90; By permission of the British Library: figs. 21 (Cott Vitt A XIII f 6), 34 (Cott Nero D II f 179v), 48 (Roy 18 E II f 401v), 49 (Roy 18 E I f 175), 54 (Roy 14 E IV f 23), 56 (Roy 16 F II f 73), 65 (1398a22 p 30), 85 (K Top LXXXIII.2), 86 (Maps 8c38), 112 (883E3 (2) 19), 120 (G12101 p 1651), 142 (Harl 1419 A f 10v), 148 (Press 1875b 35b); British Library, London, UK/Bridgeman Art Library: fig. 157; © Copyright The British Museum: figs. 61, 62 (MI I p333 No 177, GIII Ill men 473), 79 (1859-8-6-389), 109 (Pennant IX.124), 113 (Pennant IX.125), 137 (BM SAT 10854); The Trustees of the British Museum/Bridgeman Art Library: fig. 8; Cadw: Welsh Historic Monuments. Crown copyright: fig. 38; Collections/James Bartholomew: fig. 179; The Master and Fellows of Corpus Christi College, Cambridge: figs. 28, 33, 117; John Crook: fig. 30; Crown copyright: UK Government Art Collection: figs. 45, 75, 89; Crown copyright: Historic Royal Palaces: plan inside front cover (Edward Impey), half-title, figs. 3 (Ivan Lapper), 5, 9, 10, 11, 12, 13 (Ivan Lapper), 15 (Edward Impey), 16, 17, 18 (Ivan Lapper), 19, 23, 24, 26, 27, 29, 31, 32 (Ivan Lapper), 35, 36, 37, 39, 40, 41, 42, 43, 44, 47, 51, 52, 100, 102, 108, 110, 114, 118, 145, 146, 147, 149, 150, 159, 172, 173, 178; © Crown copyright. NMR: figs. 68, 72, 123, 127, 171, 175, 176; Edinburgh University Library (ms.La.III.283, fol. 346v): fig. 64; English Heritage Photographic Library: figs. 25, 106, 174; ©English Heritage. Drawing: David Honour: fig. 80; The Fotomas Index, UK: figs. 76, 105; Geary: fig. 163; © The Wardens and Commonalty of the Mystery of Goldsmiths of the City of London. All rights reserved: fig. 143; The Guildhall Library, Corporation of London: figs. 70, 96, 111, 121, 155, 162, 167; The Guildhall Library, Corporation of London, UK/Bridgeman Art Library: frontispiece, figs. 83, 93, 130, 138; Andrew Holt Photography: fig. 177; The Hulton Getty Picture Collection: fig. 66; Edward Impey: fig. 139; Peter Jackson Collection: figs. 128, 132, 165, 169, 170; London Metropolitan Archives: fig. 131; Mary Evans Picture Library: fig. 122; Jean Mesqui: fig. 14; Roy Miles Esq/Bridgeman Art Library: fig. 153; Courtesy of the Royal Mint: figs. 103, 104, 107; Musée de la Tapisserie, Bayeux, France/Bridgeman Art Library: figs. 6, 7; Museo Thyssen-Bornemisza, Madrid: fig. 57; Courtesy of the Museum of London: figs. 1, 50, 67, 95, 166; By courtesy of the National Portrait Gallery, London: figs. 98, 115, 116, 141, 144; Geoffrey Parnell: fig. 2; © Pitkin Unichrome: fig. 4; Private collection: fig. 134; The Public Record Office: figs. 69 (Work 31/123), 81 (Work 31/73), 84 (Work 31/64), 88 (Work 31/124), 94 (Work 31/129), 161 (Work 31/168), 168 (Work 31/ 494 Plan 2); The Society of Antiquaries of London: figs. 53, 55, 59, 140; Courtesy of Sotheby's Picture Library: fig. 152; The Trustees of the Victoria and Albert Museum, London: fig. 87; Christopher Wood Gallery, London, UK/Bridgeman Art Library: fig. 156.

CHAPTER OPENERS: THE TOWER IN CONTEXT (left to right)
Page 11: Geoffrey Parnell; Museo e Gallerie Nazionali di Capodimonte, Naples, Italy/Giraudon/Bridgeman Art Library; © Copyright The British Museum (OA247); Page 15: By permission of the British Library (Roy 20 A II f3), (Cott Claud B VI f124 min); Crown copyright: Historic Royal Palaces; Page 21: By permission of the British Library (Cott Claud D II f45v), (Harl 5102 f32), (Roy 20 A II f7 Det); Page 25: By permission of the British Library (Roy 16 F II f 73); British Library, London, UK/Bridgeman Art Library; Lambeth Palace Library, London, UK/Bridgeman Art Library; Page 41: Crown copyright: Historic Royal Palaces; The collection of the Duke of Buccleuch and Queensberry, KT; © The Board of Trustees of the Armouries; Page 51: By courtesy of the National Portrait Gallery, London; © National Trust Photographic Library; The Society of Antiquaries of London; Page 57: © The Board of Trustees of the Armouries; Page 61: The Fotomas Index, UK; By courtesy of the National Portrait Gallery, London; © Copyright The British Museum (Willshire Collection, Pack E.191); Page 73: Crown copyright: Historic Royal Palaces; By courtesy of the National Portrait Gallery, London; © The Board of Trustees of the Armouries; Page 83: By courtesy of the National Portrait Gallery, London; coins courtesy of the Royal Mint; Page 87: By courtesy of the National Portrait Gallery, London; Staatliche Kunstsammlungen, Kassel; © National Gallery, London; Page 91: By courtesy of the National Portrait Gallery, London; The Public Record Office (SP14/216/10); Crown copyright: Historic Royal Palaces; Page 97: By courtesy of the National Portrait Gallery, London; Crown copyright: Historic Royal Palaces; The Illustrated London News Picture Library; Page 113: By courtesy of the National Portrait Gallery, London (left and middle); Crown copyright: Historic Royal Palaces (right); Page 117: By courtesy of the National Portrait Gallery, London; RIBA Library Photographs Collection; Crown copyright: Historic Royal Palaces; Page 123: © The Board of Trustees of the Armouries; © Crown copyright. NMR; Crown copyright: Historic Royal Palaces.